PAIN

IS A

Stunning Discoveries
After Loss, Psychedelics,
and Feeling It All

PORTAL

TO

BEAUTY

ALEXIS LEIGH

Published 2025 by Jameo Publications LLC
Printed in the United States of America

Shambhala Publications Inc.: Excerpt from "Wings of Desire" from
The Pocket Rumi Reader, edited by Kabir Helminski. Reprinted by
arrangement with The Permissions Company, LLC on behalf of
Shambhala Publications Inc., Boulder, Colorado, Shambhala.com.

Publisher's Cataloging-in-Publication Data
Names: Leigh, Alexis, author.
Title: Pain is a portal to beauty: stunning discoveries after loss,
psychedelics, and feeling it all / Alexis Leigh.
Identifiers: LCCN 2025905108 | ISBN 979-8-9927420-1-5 (hardback) |
ISBN 979-8-9927420-0-8 (paperback) | ISBN 979-8-9927420-2-2 (ebook)
Subjects: LCSH: Leigh, Alexis. | Psychic trauma. | Grief. | Hallucinogenic
drugs—Therapeutic use. | Self-actualization (Psychology). | Divorced
Women—United States—Biography. | BISAC: BIOGRAPHY &
AUTOBIOGRAPHY / Memoirs | BODY, MIND & SPIRIT / Healing | SELF-
HELP / Personal Growth / General | FAMILY & RELATIONSHIPS / General
Classification: LCC RC552.P67 .L45 2025 | DDC 616.85/21—dc23

Cover design by Kam Bains
Interior design by Lieve Maas
Author photo by Becca Blevins Photography

This book is dedicated to all those who held things with me, for me, until I could hold them alone.

Contents

Reflections

Pain Is a Portal to Beauty

Introduction

"If you die today, your life will have been a tragedy."

This was the message I heard from a mysterious voice while walking in the woods one day during the summer of 2020. On the surface, it seemed like a ridiculous assertion.

I was an Ivy League graduate. I landed one of the top investment banking jobs after leaving Wharton. After banking, I went on to effortlessly form my own consulting practice, which paid well and allowed me full autonomy and an enviable work-life balance. I married the captain of Penn's soccer team, a man whose goodness cannot be overstated. We had a joyful, delightful four-year-old son. We lived in a lovely home within a tight-knit community, and we had wonderful friends. We all had our health. And, while I lost my mom when I was young, I was close with my dad and my sisters. My husband's family was fun and warm and loving. In a world that seemed to be crumbling around me, I had what felt like an embarrassment of riches.

But the voice in the woods revealed a secret I had been desperately trying to avoid: These riches were covering up profound sadness. Sadness laced with heartbreak from losing my mom. Sadness laced with loneliness in the way I experienced my marriage and the world around me. Sadness laced with resignation—that what I had, that what I knew, was all there is.

My life didn't fit me anymore after the voice in the woods. Pieces started falling away. I slowly started letting go of my business. I had rounds and rounds of friendships falling away. With busy lives, this could happen rather gently, ramping down contact over time. But the biggest pieces, the most important ones, fell away like a glacier calving. My marriage. *Crash.* My relationships with my family. *Boom.* In an instant, what had just been something connected, integral, a part of me, was gone, leaving a vast nothingness in its stead.

I needed the nothingness.

To sit in the dark and the quiet.

To cut away the ties to those in my life so I could melt away the person I had been.

It was in the nothingness that I would find my way to my teachers. To the authors and healers who would start to awaken things within me. To psychedelics, which would—sometimes playfully, sometimes terrifyingly—shine the light so I could see. To a new love interest, a man who would act as a relentless mirror for me as I tried to piece together who I am.

It was in the nothingness that I would plumb the depths of my pain. Frightening pain, harrowing pain, more pain than I ever imagined was there.

But it was also in the nothingness that I would start to come alive. To come alive in a way I do not remember during this lifetime. Every time I journeyed into the darkness, every time I immersed myself in my pain, I came out the other side with an astonishing treasure. I found out I am a writer after a lifetime of thinking I was terrible with words. I found out I am a talented burlesque dancer after feeling too timid to even dance by myself. I found out I have a powerful coloratura soprano singing voice after being too embarrassed to even sing in the shower.

I found out that everything I ever dreamt of, once rejected as fanciful, was meant to be. I am destined to live a life filled with awe and beauty and love.

I wonder how many are living tragic lives like the one I lived for so long. With uncovered gifts, with a deficiency of love, with resignation that this is all there is, rather than trusting their resistance—*there has to be more.*

Unaware that the *more* they crave is not something out there but right here, parts of themselves they have shut down entirely to avoid their pain. Unspeakably beautiful parts, parts they unconsciously miss in every moment of every day. Parts that, once rediscovered, will change the world.

This is my story, as well as I can recall, as best as I can tell it. And it is just that—a story. A series of understandings of happenings, understandings that shift within these pages and surely will continue to shift for years to come.

At the end of this book, you'll find a collection of reflections, pieces of my story that fall outside the confines of my initial journey but that contribute to the sense of spaciousness, of warmth, of hopefulness as we continue the work of finding out who we are and what this is all about.

I am aware that my path is distinctly my own, so I share this story not to tell anyone what to do but to try to relay the truth, love, and aliveness I have found in case it sparks truth, love, and aliveness in another.

If this sharing can help you, I'm delighted. If it can reflect back to you some of your own divinity, what a gift to us all.

Three Weeks

My dad left early for church because he taught Sunday school, and we'd follow later in my mom's car. When church was over, it was always a race to see who would get home first—"I'm going with Mom!" "I'm going with Dad!" The day we learned our mom was going to rehab, in late fall of 1992, all three blonde-haired, blue-eyed girls piled into my mom's teal sedan after church. I had just turned eleven, and my sisters were thirteen and fifteen. When we got into the car, my mom told us she and my dad wanted to talk with us about something when we got home.

I remember feeling embarrassed and kicking my sister's seat in front of me, confident she had told them I needed to start wearing deodorant, that this was the subject matter for the day. I have a hard time accessing other details, like what I was wearing, what the interior of the car looked like, whether it was hot or cold that day. I don't remember with any specificity what my parents actually shared with us when we got home. I just remember hearing that my mom was sick and that she was going away for three weeks.

What I know now is that my mother was addicted to prescription drugs in the benzodiazepine family. She was prescribed medications like Valium to treat her depression. Once she became addicted, she took advantage of the lack of integration in the prescription drug system at the time and went to multiple doctors to satisfy her addiction. She also stole prescription medication from others and had alcohol hidden around the house.

But back then, I had no context for addiction and was oblivious to the tragic possibilities ahead. All I could understand was that my mom was going away for three weeks, and that alone felt like a devastating impossibility for me. I struggled intensely with separation anxiety. First-day-of-school pictures show my two happy sisters and a sobbing me. When I went to a friend's house for a sleepover, I invariably called my parents at bedtime, talking in code about how I felt sick to my stomach, asking if they could please come get me. How was I going to make it three weeks without the person whose absence I couldn't tolerate for a day?

After we dropped her off at the Dallas Fort Worth airport, crying in the bucket seats of our silver minivan, my sister and I gripped each other's hands tightly. We would get through this together. Three weeks.

But three weeks bled into more weeks. At some point we visited my mom while she was in rehab at Hazelden in Minnesota. I don't remember seeing her much, as we spent a bunch of time attending Al-Anon meetings and learning about her addiction. I do remember feeling really uncomfortable there. Like everyone was looking at me, wanting something from me. Someone even asked me to present them with their sobriety coin. In reality, I am sure they were just sad for me, the youngest person in attendance, wanting to embrace me and give me love. But I didn't want their love. All I wanted was my mom.

In the small windows where I did get to see her—to sit in her lap, in her embrace—I melted in the warmth I had missed and needed so much. I was home. But two days later, as we drove away and Hazelden disappeared from view, my home was ripped away from me once more. With no sense for our next reunion, nothing could soothe my broken heart. So my body's natural defense mechanism kicked in and numbed the pain of my mom's absence so I could survive.

And the hits kept on coming, so there was no reason for the numbing to stop. During the eighteen months after she left for rehab, my mom went from Hazelden to the Mayo Clinic to a halfway house to an apartment to extended family members' homes to homeless shelters. In June of 1994, my mom went missing, so my dad hired a private investigator to find her. There was a body discovered in a North Texas field, decomposed to such an extent that the cause of death could not be determined. But the dental records were a match: It was my mom.

That late fall Sunday turned out to be my mom's last ride home with us. The next time I was at the church with her, she was in a closed casket at the front of the sanctuary, and I felt nothing. During the funeral, I put my hand on my father's back in support, which caused him to start whimpering. I felt deep compassion for his heartbreak, but I did not have my own. I went through the motions, dutifully finding my place in the receiving line and accepting condolences with the expected grace of a young Texan lady, now twelve years old.

A month or two after the funeral, I looked at myself in the large, wood-trimmed mirror in my bedroom, trying to access the grief of losing my mother. I held a pair of scissors up to my throat, as if I should want to stab myself to put an end to the unbearable pain. I tried to cry, but I couldn't because my grief was manufactured, a fictionalized version of what I knew I should be feeling. I observed this unfeeling actor in the mirror with utter confusion. Why can't I feel anything? What is wrong with me?

The Voice

I moved through life with the sense that my mom's death didn't affect me much. I'd have isolated moments of recognition, of sadness. But I didn't know what it was like to have a mom then, so there wasn't something for me to miss, I thought.

I went ahead to excel in academics and extracurriculars, supported by my father and following the path blazed by my sisters. In high school, I was captain of the soccer team, president of several organizations, a cheerleader, a member of the jazz band, part of the student body leadership. I won awards for academics and soccer and my piano playing. My dad made me stay home from the Thanksgiving ski trip my senior year to finish my college essays, and it paid off. I

9

ultimately had my pick between Princeton and Penn, and I chose to attend Penn.

I met my husband during the spring semester of his senior year and my junior year at Penn. I've got a thing for soccer players, so he was on my radar. Apparently I was on his, too, as he joined a community service effort I organized to meet me. A native Oregonian, he showed up to the first meeting wearing khakis and hiking boots, cementing my image of people who just walk in the woods all day. Since I was from Texas, he assumed I rode a horse to school. We managed to overcome our stereotypes and slowly, shyly started courting each other. Our first date was not labeled as such—I had asked him for some pointers on my upcoming trip to Spain because he had studied there, and he said we could get together to talk about it.

I was not a big drinker and made the mistake of having a glass of wine at an event just before our dinner "meeting," so I showed up tipsy and uncharacteristically chatty, spilling my drink as we walked to our table. He was intrigued by my being a vegetarian, as his mother and stepmother were both vegetarians. He told me that he, too, planned to become a vegetarian. Each year, over a period of seven years, he would drop a meat-eating day of the week. *Alright*, I thought in my buzzed state, *this guy's got a plan*.

After our dinner, we walked around campus, and I stopped to buy a candy bar from a young boy who was fundraising. I'd later learn how much my husband loved that I regularly stopped to support strangers like this. He'd later learn how much I loved candy. We ended up going back to his apartment to find something to watch and bizarrely landed on the famously long *Dances with Wolves*. We sat there for the entire three hours like total strangers, our knees barely touching. Only when the credits started to roll did we turn toward each other, press our foreheads together, and start making out.

As enamored as I was with this way-cute soccer player, I saw this as a fling, so we hung out for a couple of months until he graduated. Then we said, "See ya!" and he drove across the country to Oregon.

But we kept in touch and ended up visiting each other a couple of times that summer. During my visit to Portland, I fell for him. There were so many things I loved about him. He expanded my world, showing me adventure and beauty that I had not known before. He adored me, but he was also willing to gently, playfully poke at me when my perspective needed a little widening. He was strong and steady, which let him be patient and kind. His persistent calm soothed my nervous system. And he's hilarious. People who know him can't *not* comment on what a good guy he is.

We moved to San Francisco when I graduated, but my husband's heart was always set on returning to Oregon. So after a couple of years, we left the Bay Area, took a short detour to Maui, and then headed up north to his hometown, Portland. A few years later came our precious son.

My husband and I felt very fortunate to be with someone we trusted and admired. We had a blast adventuring together. We knew we were lucky to have flexibility in our careers, supporting each other's entrepreneurial efforts and able to dial up or down the work to spend time with our son.

And, as with any marriage, we had our challenges. We struggled to negotiate both of our needs amidst the complexities of work and parenting and family obligations. I wished for more time together, for more connection, to be reassured of his love for me. And I think he yearned for more space and for peace—to feel settled in our love for each other, to be grateful for what was instead of trying to make things other than what they were. Despite some painful dynamics, we had the winning ingredients: We loved each other, we shared a beautiful son, and we were both willing to work on the relationship. What else could you possibly ask for?

———

When I was thirty-eight, I went for a walk in the woods one summer afternoon while our son was napping. And that's when I heard the voice:

"If you die today, your life will have been a tragedy."

It's not like I looked around to see who said it—the words came from within me. I was not a spiritual person at this time in my life, and I didn't know whose words they were, but there was not an ounce of resistance. Amidst the towering cedars, my body went limp and the tears began to flow.

I was not depressed. I easily found moments of joy and laughter with loved ones. I delighted in our four-year-old son. I did want more happiness, more ease, more meaning, more love in my life. And I had endless energy to get out of bed each day and keep working, working, working toward this goal. I went to therapy, read books, processed with loved ones, and looked constantly for all the ways to improve my life.

But I was heartbroken. And my marriage was where I felt this acutely. I loved my husband with all of my heart, as I believe he loved me. We just didn't know how to receive each other's love. We were pouring our love into leaky buckets. So we both constantly felt misunderstood, unseen, and unloved. All I could hear was that he wanted to escape me. And all he could hear, I think, was that he would never be enough. We were at the brink of giving up many times, but each time we'd find it in us to keep going. To lose him and to break up our family was more than I thought I could bear. I clung to the promise that one day we'd get there. We had to.

That moment in the woods was a loving tap on the shoulder to let me know I was not getting there. It was terrifying to entertain that the cherished pieces that composed my life might be the wrong ones. But, as a hurt child holds in tears until they see Mom or Dad and can safely release, I finally felt understood for the depth of my grief and could surrender to it.

Of course, the heartbreak did not originate with my marriage. It was just the container to showcase this, to present me with the opportunity to heal from the loss of my mom—to her depression, to her addiction, to rehab, and ultimately to her death. I buried the pain from these experiences deep within, but I knew now that I had to start the excavation work. It was time to wake up so I could do more than survive.

But how to dig up those memories? I didn't make a conscious decision to bury them—it was my body's natural defense mechanism to keep me alive. So it's not like I could just say, *Cool, I'm ready to remember*. In my years of therapy, when we would touch upon a particularly painful subject, I would feel the wave of numbing, starting from my toes and moving its way to my head. I could not control it. And our work for the day was over because I couldn't feel anything anymore.

What I found was that accessing memories was more effective when done by myself. Someone else's participation or reaction would interrupt my process and bring on the numbing. So I put on sad music and went for walks. Max Richter's "On the Nature of Daylight" brought on instant tears. Some memories were from when I was too young, so I had to imagine what it felt like and go with what resonated. Brick by brick, the picture started to come together.

I tapped into the desperation I experienced as a newborn, crying out for love and attention and withdrawing in hopelessness when my depressed mother didn't come. I tapped into the inexplicable, pervasive fear I had as a young girl that I would be permanently separated from my mom. During one of her trips abroad when I was maybe seven years old, I stood alone at our kitchen bay window in my light blue nightgown, tears streaming silently down my face. Staring out at the night sky, I was keenly aware that someday she might not come home.

I tapped into the piercing loneliness I felt throughout childhood and how I felt crushed under more responsibility than I could possibly handle. How could I both explore my place in the world and manage my life as a caring, capable, wise parent would? I did not have that capacity or wisdom.

So I had to wing it. I had to grit my teeth and get through. Sitting on a brick pillar outside my school, stranded long after everyone else had gone home, I scanned my surroundings constantly for potential dangers. I carried intense shame for showing up imperfectly, like having more than my fair share of dental cavities, when the building blocks of my life were the diet and hygiene of a neglected child. And in a desperate attempt to keep her safe and happy, I tried to shield my mom from her own embarrassment and shame, running interference with friends' parents, apologizing to her when I had company over and she walked through the house in her underwear.

Then came the heartbreak and resignation when my worst nightmare came true.

Nearly three decades later, I was standing on a gravel path of Portland's tree-lined Wilshire Park when the eleven-year-old part of me woke up and realized my mother never came home. Doubled over and weeping, I screamed out in agony, "Three weeks! They said she'd be gone for three weeks!"

One day my life's trajectory came into view: from my grandfather, who died by suicide—to my mother's tragic demise—to me and my forty years of heartache and loneliness—to the life that awaited my son. It seemed so obvious. Of course my life was the outgrowth of this legacy of tragedy.

This voice in the woods interrupted my life to let me know I could break this cycle.

Getting Clear

Over the years, as I would share my marital struggles with loved ones, they would ask why I stayed in the marriage. It was like they were speaking in a foreign language—what on earth do you mean? After losing my mother, I could not fathom how you could *choose* to walk away from the person you loved most in the world.

But the voice in the woods fundamentally altered my perspective—there was a greater tragedy at play than losing my husband. The day I heard the voice, I texted my best friend, "I don't want to be on my deathbed having lived my life this lonely."

So a few months after the voice, my husband and I decided to separate. I was devastated. I was terrified for the impact on our son. And—I was emboldened. I could not take one more step in the same direction if I wanted to change my life's trajectory.

My husband and I both stayed in the house, and we were open to a reconciliation, but after so many years of struggle, I wasn't hopeful. So I began to "try on" getting divorced. I sketched out a parenting schedule so that we could reduce tension in the presence of our son and so that I could see what I was getting into for that potential next phase. I looked at my finances from the perspective of a single parent and began talking with companies about working for them full-time so I could have a more predictable income than what my project-based consulting business provided. I reached out to other divorced women to see what it was like, and one recommended I read *Codependent No More* by Melody Beattie.

This book blew my mind. In my marriage, I was always waiting for the someday scenario. Someday things will click, things will be better, we will be connected, I will feel loved. This made the decision to leave the relationship impossible. I don't have all of the information—it could be better just around the corner. From *Codependent No More*, I learned that someday is not where I should be living. I should be living in the today. I have the information I need. So I began to change my lens from rose-colored to clear. No more sugarcoating or wishful projection. I want to look at what's real.

—

The door to my detached garage has an audible noise when opened and shut as the weather stripping rubs against the threshold. My husband used the garage as his home office, and because of this noise I could hear anytime he was coming into the house, where I worked upstairs. Every time I heard that noise, my heart would lift in anticipation. It wasn't fully conscious, but there was a longing—maybe this time he would come upstairs to say hi, to want to spend some time together, to offer connection. I've stumbled upon journals where I became aware that I would listen for his footsteps. I deeply longed for more closeness with him.

It is obvious now, but I didn't realize then how much my mother's absence affected the ways I looked for connection with my husband. In her book *Emotional Inheritance*, Galit Atlas talks about emotionally absent mothers, explaining that the child of a so-called "dead mother" will do anything to connect with their mom, to try to bring her back to life. She writes, "When the child gives up on bringing their mother back to life, they will try to restore the connection through the renunciation of their own aliveness. They will meet the mother in her deadness and thus will develop their own emotional deadness." This was me. After school, instead of exploring the world and discovering more of myself, I sat with my sleeping, drugged mother to create the picture of closeness, to assure myself that I was connected to the person I loved and needed most in the world.

And I continued to tell myself this story after she died, with my husband as her proxy. I tried tirelessly to create a closeness that was not there. I downplayed critical needs of mine as unimportant because they could not be met in this relationship.

As I began to see the link between how I related to my mom and to my husband, I would visualize myself in the North Texas field where my mother died, sitting next to her lifeless body, pleading with her to wake up. I would say to myself, *Alexis, she is not going to wake up. You need to stop looking there.*

And I started to become honest about the missing pieces in my marriage. The connection I desired hadn't come in nearly two decades, and there wasn't any reason to believe that would change. *Alexis, he is not coming upstairs. You need to stop looking there.*

The Kitchen Table

My struggles in relationship were not limited to my marriage. Up to this point in time, my mantra was basically "People suck." For the most part, I could not find my way to relationships that felt nurturing and reciprocal. After reading *Codependent No More* and Katherine Woodward Thomas's *Calling in "The One,"* I learned that I was responsible for what felt disappointing in my relationships.

I don't mean that it was my fault.

My childhood was brutal, I did nothing to deserve it, and the patterns I had in relationship were the logical, unavoidable outgrowth of the protective mechanisms I developed to survive. It's just that now I can tap into power I wasn't able to access as a defenseless child.

In my relationships, I felt victim to others not treating me as I desired—others didn't care for me, didn't show up for me, didn't celebrate me in the way I deserved. What I learned was that I also didn't take care of myself and that I regularly abandoned myself to qualify for another's affection. And, having disappeared myself in these relationships, there was no self to believe in or celebrate.

I would drop everything if someone needed me. I would automatically agree to plans based on another's needs without checking in to make sure my needs were taken care of as well. Even in big decisions—like where we would live or where I went to law school—I felt my needs were entirely unimportant relative to my husband's.

I wanted to go to New York for law school. I was excited about Columbia's rigorous program and thrilled for the chance to live in the same city as my best friend after several years away. But I knew my husband (then boyfriend) wanted to stay in Portland. He was from there, his family all lived there, and it was his intention to end up there. He had tried for years to persuade me to move to Portland, and I felt resistance from him about moving away, especially with big unknowns like what he would do for work. But I didn't have the courage to press it, to see if it was possible to honor both of us. I saw it as a choice between my relationship and my career aspirations, and I wasn't willing to risk the former. So I squashed my dreams and went to law school in Portland. It was an unmatchable sacrifice, and the resentment that followed was huge and devastating to our relationship.

I developed these destructive tendencies because I was starved for love and thought I could only get love from others. When I was young, I was in the practice of sitting at our kitchen table—a central location within our home— in the hopes that I would intersect with my father to get some quality time together. He was a single dad, community leader, and busy lawyer, and I would try to catch him so we could chat for a couple of minutes as he was walking out the door or in the car on his five-minute ride to work. And now I realized that I was firmly in this practice as an adult. I so feared missing out on the love I desperately needed from others if I went and did my own thing.

I decided I was not settling for crumbs anymore. I didn't quite know how things would unfold, but I knew I had to leave the kitchen table.

So I started to accept responsibility and began to exercise this new muscle. I did not let myself answer the phone or respond to a text until I could truly say that I wanted to be in contact at that time. After a friend routinely forgot my birthday, I let myself off the hook for hers. I stopped reaching for the check at every meal, challenging myself to become honest about whether I was being generous or whether this gesture was actually motivated by a subconscious belief that I owed others.

And I tried to slow down and check in about my needs more regularly. One time I was at the grocery store, grabbing provisions for a loved one who was in the middle of a very busy workweek. As I was scanning the protein bar selection, it dawned on me to ask myself, *Do you want a bar too?* Mounds of tension left my body, so relieved to be seen for my needs too.

As I slowed down, as I stopped the over-giving, as I brought my attention and energy back to me, the need for others to treat me in a certain way began to fade into the background. I became clear that it was *my* neglect of me, *my* abandonment of me that was heart-wrenching, and my relationships were simply reflecting that neglect back to me. And my care for me began to fill me up. I didn't feel as lonely anymore.

I realized I wasn't missing others, I was missing myself.

Fortieth Birthday

My college girlfriends live in New York, and we get together every few years for a girls' weekend. In anticipation of my fortieth birthday, we planned to meet up in Southern California. A year into the pandemic, I was still pretty anxious about getting Covid, so when I heard that one of my friends proactively tested prior to the trip, I followed suit and signed up for a drive-through test in Portland a couple of days before I flew out. Unfortunately, I did not get the results by the time I left for my trip. *(Ominous music plays here.)*

We flew in on a Thursday and headed out for dinner at a cute, trendy restaurant in Newport Beach. It was so soothing to be able to catch up live with these dear, longtime friends with the luxury of having all weekend ahead of us. You just can't catch up enough via text, and the occasional phone call always had a time pressure with busy lives and time zone differences.

We talked about our work, our kids, our husbands. I unemotionally shared that my husband and I were close to calling it quits. Ten months into our separation, things weren't getting any better. They shared how much they loved their husbands and—despite the ups and downs of marriage—how they couldn't imagine life without them. I didn't look to my girlfriends' relationships to tell me whether my relationship was okay. But at times it was helpful to hear their experience to have some context for whether the "hard" I experienced in my marriage was the right level of hard, the right kind of hard.

The next morning we headed to breakfast at the hotel restaurant. And while I was enjoying my avocado toast on the patio, I got the email. Wide-eyed, I slowly reached for my mask and said, "Guys, I have Covid."

I did not have Covid. The testing site I had used was super sketch. I'd watched them use the same plastic gloves to collect each sample. So someone else's Covid likely got on my swab, or they mixed up the results altogether, who knows. But I could not prove that it was a false positive in time to save my trip. My friends were so gracious—and unconcerned, confident it was a false positive given what I relayed about the testing site—but we played it safe. There was a frenzy of activity between securing testing and rental cars and making phone calls to family members and people whom I had potentially exposed. I heard my girlfriends' conversations with their husbands, who desperately did not want them to get stuck in California—"Come home!"

After my twenty-plus hour drive back to Portland, still awaiting reliable confirmation that I did not have Covid, my family and I sat in our backyard, distanced and masked. I asked about their weekend, and my husband outlined all of the things he had gotten done while I was away, stating that he was so glad I was gone so he could get so much done. All I could hear was that my friends' husbands desired their prompt return and my husband was so glad I was gone.

I know my friends' husbands urgently wanted them home at least in part because of the logistical nightmare that would ensue if they got stuck across the country with Covid. And I know my husband did not mean any unkindness with his statement. But the juxtaposition triggered deep sadness in me that, throughout my life, those I loved didn't desire my presence. I don't have a single memory of walking through the door in my childhood home where someone was there to welcome me, glad I was home. And this is how I felt in my marriage the bulk of the time—I would have loved to have felt missed, I would have settled to have felt needed. But I mostly felt like a burden.

I knew our marriage had little life left in it. But that didn't keep my heart from breaking once more. Looking across at the man I loved with all my heart, hidden by my mask, tears streamed down my cheeks.

The Decision

During the last few months of our counseling sessions, there was no major movement. It was like a slow, gentle process of letting the last of the air out of the tire. So when we formally decided to divorce, it was a calm and mutual decision.

On a warm, sunny day while our son was at school, I asked my husband, "Hey, can we talk?"

"Sure."

We moved to the living room—I sat on the light blue couch, and he sat opposite me on the off-white leather reading chair. We were casually dressed in our usual attire of jeans and T-shirts, and my husband leaned forward, curious as to the subject matter of this meeting.

I felt grounded and openhearted as I began. "We have struggled for so long. And things aren't getting better. I wonder how it would feel to just honor that? To honor that we are both validly where we are, and that those two places simply aren't aligned right now?"

My husband's shoulders dropped, his eyes softened. He said, "I appreciate your framing it that way. That feels right to me."

He seemed relieved. I was too. We could set down this heavy load with gratitude and respect for all that we had worked tirelessly to create. We could see our separation as the loving path forward instead of calling it a failure or saying that we were wrong somehow.

In our many years of couples counseling, my husband and I would appear to have the occasional breakthrough, but, like a rock rolled uphill, there was a gravitational pull back into our natural resting place of incompatibility. At some point I realized that when I thought we had a breakthrough, it was just *me* talking to *me* and convincing *me* that we were making progress. Believing I understood our dynamics better, I presumed that we both had a new understanding that would translate to more connection. A branch off my dissociative tendencies: I was unconsciously playing pretend in lieu of sitting with my hopelessness.

Our therapist's hypothesis, as I understood it, was that if we just healed our childhood trauma enough, our issues would resolve—we would be happy together. In *The Drama of the Gifted Child*, Alice Miller writes that the therapist "is in danger of behaving like a friend who brings a good meal to a prisoner in his cell, at the precise moment when that prisoner has the chance to escape—perhaps to spend his first night hungry and without shelter—but in freedom nevertheless." We had the opportunity to bravely and compassionately look at who we were and what we most wanted in life. But the singular goal of our counseling sessions was to keep us together, intolerant of curiosity, dismissing our unhappiness as stemming entirely from our trauma, missing the beauty of our individual souls and what filled us up.

Author Dan Millman writes, "The secret of change is to focus all of your energy, not on fighting the old, but on building the new." After nineteen years of fighting the old, I was ready to set down those tools and come from a place of creativity instead of reactivity. The question for me transformed from *Can I keep going*? to *What am I here to do*?

No one could know my internal experience, and as long as I looked externally—to therapists, friends, family, belief systems—I made choices that didn't honor me. It wasn't until the voice in the woods that I realized I had to start listening to me.

Really, I was getting guidance long before that voice. In every instance of heartbreak, in every moment of hopelessness, there were important messages for me. *You are here to love and be loved. You have immense power to change your life.* The wisdom was within me all along. I just didn't yet know how to listen.

After our living-room conversation, my husband and I walked to school to pick up our son. There was a lightness to our energy together, an ease that came with this brand-new experience of honoring each other for who we were, where we were. Of course, I couldn't have understood in that moment all of the pain that was waiting for me as we moved forward with our divorce. But there was an air of possibility, a feeling of aliveness, as we took this step off the well-worn path into the unknown.

Solitude

My father, my sisters, and I had been very close since my mom died. It was the silver lining of her loss. But that closeness sprang from an acute awareness of the potential for things to fall apart, of the potential for devastating loss, so it had a tight grip that ultimately drained all of us. It involved being there for each other, no matter what, any time. Any one of us would have jumped on a plane (and did) if the other was struggling. If someone called, we answered.

Our unspoken motto was that you show up, and we did—we were there for each other, commonly at the expense of our own needs. And, frankly, we sometimes showed up because we thought the other needed it when they actually didn't. Sacrifice + insufficient gratitude =

wads of resentment. Between my divorce, another family member's health crisis, and everyone's overwhelm—Covid-related and otherwise—we were done. We all needed space from each other.

Now I was alone. Sure, I had good friends and loved ones who would take my call if I needed them but not the kind where I'd call them any time without hesitation. And I rarely reached out, in part not to burden them and in part because the material was too tender. There was no wiggle room—I couldn't risk getting a response that didn't perfectly hold what I was going through. I would go for days, some-times weeks, engulfed in sorrow—about my marriage, about my childhood, about things I couldn't name. In the darkest stretches, I worried that it may be more than I could handle. I had weekly therapy sessions with my psychedelic guide, but sometimes I was not sure how I could make it to our next session. I would put my six-year-old son to bed and watch him sleep, terrified for this precious, vulnerable child whose mother was too close to the edge.

So I did things to interrupt the pain and to fill my soul. I went to dance class, I went for runs in the forest, I went paddleboarding on the river, I chased sunsets, and I turned on stand-up comedy (I love you, Fortune Feimster). As soon as the activity was over, my pain was there knocking. But the break—and the movement, the beauty, the laughter—gave me enough energy to keep going. I would talk candidly with my son about how both his needs and my needs were important. And how we'd do lots of fun things he liked, but we also needed to take care of Mommy's soul, so we were going to hike and spend time in nature.

My guide often remarked how brave I was, proceeding down this healing path with such courage when I didn't have a support team. Can it be brave when you don't see it as a choice? But being on my own was a superpower I developed as a kid, and that lack of support ended up leading to rapid healing after feeling stuck for so long. In *Letting Go*, David Hawkins says that the way to truly heal is to sit with emotions—not suppress, escape, or even express them to others. Sharing emotions with loved ones, as I did for years, did not allow me to release them. For me, it was a way to avoid being immersed in the emotion, and it remained stuck, ready to come up again at the next trigger. When I stayed with an emotion, feeling it fully without analysis or manipulation, it could finally leave my body.

This is not an all-or-nothing proposition. It's just that the more I sit with an emotion, the more I listen, the more healing I get. But, given that my trauma was being utterly alone when I desperately needed others, I have sometimes worried that meditation and sitting alone with an intense emotion may not always be the right call. It could further my trauma to force myself down a path that is too much for me to travel alone. Hawkins concedes that in overwhelm we do, in fact, need to consciously use a coping mechanism to reduce the magnitude of the emotion, to break it into bite-size, digestible pieces. So I sometimes may need a tether— as my guide provided—to help me as I bring some of the darkest pieces into the light.

And sometimes I need to stop feeling for a minute. One night I was listening to cello cover songs, and I heard a cover of "Señorita." A scene formed in my head where I was dancing my last dance with my husband before we changed partners. It made me so desperately sad.

When I later shared my overwhelm with my guide, she said to turn off the cello covers and turn on the polka music.

So I did.

And I made it another day.

~~Psycha~~ ~~Psycho~~ Psychedelics

During the same summer when I heard the voice in the woods, I received a request to create a business plan for an educational institution that trains psychedelic guides. Having zero background or context in this area, I can't tell you how many times I misspelled the word *psychedelics* in their financial model. I did not know anyone who had personally used psychedelics. I had not yet been exposed to Michael Pollan's *How to Change Your Mind*, and I was not following the science or the efforts toward legality. I didn't even know the names of the psychedelics—or that there was more than one kind!

After my mom died, I made a commitment to never do drugs. I was the proud, outspoken leader of my middle school's DARE (Drug Abuse Resistance Education) program, and, following through on my thirteen-year-old commitment, I stayed away from drugs completely. Given the potential for a genetic predisposition to drug addiction, I was hesitant to even take over-the-counter pain medicine.

But working with this educational institution started to pique my curiosity. The people I worked with were so lovely and so committed to helping others find healing, having experienced such profound healing themselves. Around the time my co-parent and I decided to divorce, I called a life coach to bounce some ideas off of her amidst all the change in my life. She thought I might find value in using psychedelics as part of my healing journey.

Up to that point, in my many years of talk therapy, I was fortunate to have warm, loving, intelligent, deeply compassionate women as therapists. They were gentle guides, patient with me as I resisted looking at the painful pieces of my life. They would go above and beyond, making space for me when I had emergencies, when I was in deep grief about my marriage. There was never the express comparison to being a mother figure for me, but it felt a little like that. They took me under their wing, guarding me and my fragile state as I began to wake up to my pain.

By the time I talked with my psychedelic guide, I was ready for a different kind of guidance. I now had the ability to protect myself, to hold myself with the gentleness and warmth bestowed on me by my previous therapists, and I was ready to take my healing up a level. To do whatever I needed to make a huge change in my life. On my intake form, I wrote that I wanted "increased awareness, healing, and integration—to change my family's trajectory of tragedy for myself and my son."

When I first talked with my guide via Zoom, I was struck by her immense capacity for compassion and her skill and knowledge base around trauma work. She talked about my trauma with precision, introducing me to new frameworks and delving more deeply into material than I had before. She gave me the primer on psychedelics, which have long been used by indigenous cultures for healing and spiritual practices.

Psychedelics are experiencing a mainstream revitalization for their therapeutic potential in treating conditions such as depression, anxiety, and PTSD. Known for their consciousness-altering properties, psychedelics activate serotonin receptors in the brain, thereby enhancing neural plasticity to help us rewire, disrupting deeply ingrained patterns and allowing newer, healthier patterns to develop. Those who use psychedelics come away with an altered sense of self and increased feelings of connectedness.

———

My approach to psychedelics was the same as my approach to my middle school crushes. On the last day of fifth grade, wearing a light green fitted top, knee-length cutoff jean shorts, white socks, and loafers, I walked across the blacktop to ask Mark Johnson to "go with me." He said yes. I would continue to fearlessly ask boys out for years to come, much to the bewilderment of friends who wouldn't dare take that kind of risk. Maybe it's less that I was fearless and more that my desire to be connected to these cute boys was so much louder than my fear of rejection.

That's how psychedelics felt to me. When I have shared with people about my journeys, some say, "I could never let go of control like that." I just didn't have that kind of resistance. First, I have generally been able to trust my gut about things. I see the high-level picture, I can pick up on energy, I can tell early on if a situation is safe or not. I knew deep down I could trust the process and the people I was working with. But I also had something much louder than the fear of surrendering control—I heard my life was a tragedy. The risk of psychedelics paled in comparison to the risk of doing nothing. There was an urgency to change my life so that I didn't leave my son like my mom left me, so that he wouldn't be condemned to a life of loneliness and sadness. Using psychedelics was my Hail Mary as the clock was ticking down.

Of course, I checked the boxes with my guide.

"What's the risk of addiction?" None.

"I'm getting a divorce. Should I wait and call you in six or twelve months when things settle a bit?" She said we could wait, but it could also be the perfect time as the medicine would help me work through the myriad of emotions that were surfacing.

I countered, "Okay, but I am a single mom now. And my son is going through a huge transition. I have to show up for him. This can't crack me open such that I can't be there for him." She reassured me that because of all of the internal work I'd done, I would be okay. Those who see their worlds turn upside down tend to have had little introspection before working with the medicines. And I would have her support as I integrated the journeys on the backside.

I was also curious about the whole "everyone is connected" concept I'd heard about. If I came to understand that we are all connected, that we are all one, would I become relatively less connected to my son? Would my love for him lessen in comparison as my love for all of humanity grew? It terrified me that I could come to a place where I'd be less attached to being there with and for my son. My guide reassured me that it was the opposite—this work intensifies the love we feel for those in our lives.

"Any more questions?"

"When can we start?"

Wholly Blissful

We did several intake sessions in preparation for my first guided journey. This was all happening in the same month when my co-parent moved out of the house, so I had lots of emotions to work with.

It felt like my life was falling apart, and I had no vision for how it would come back together, whether it *could* come back together. I felt irreparably broken from my trauma. I believed that not having a mother's love in the one life I had to live cost me the chance to have a happy partnership during this one life. It cost my son the chance to have a happy childhood during his one life. Instead of having the large, vibrant family and community I longed for, mine was unraveling, plagued by painful patterns, disconnection, and distance. I hoped psychedelics might help me find peace with my brokenness.

My guide supported me through these issues during the preparation sessions, and we started to formulate an intention for this first journey. A couple of the themes were finding clarity around my relationship with my co-parent and strengthening the belief that I am worthy of love.

As I mentioned, I have generally been able to trust my gut, so I didn't do exhaustive research before my first journey, relying on my guide for the relevant information. Well, it turns out I may have missed a detail or two in our intake discussions. In the first few minutes of my journey, when I was blissfully feeling the medicine, I said something about psilocybin, and my guide responded, "You're not on psilocybin, you're on Molly!"

I erupted in laughter and squawked, "I need to send out a newsletter! I told everyone I was doing mushrooms today!"

For those of you who are also new to this acronym, MDMA (3,4-Methylenedioxymethamphetamine) is a psychedelic drug also known as Ecstasy or Molly. MDMA induces feelings of empathy and euphoria and lowers the fear response so that the patient can access trauma with less overwhelm and stress. What I know now is that a common practice is to start with MDMA to help the patient work through ego-level trauma before approaching the ego dissolution—the loss of one's sense of self—associated with psilocybin.

During the journey, I was lying on a couch, eyes covered, listening to a playlist curated by my guide, and all I felt was an exquisite vibration. I had no anxiety, no loneliness, no pain. I just was. My guide recorded some of my insights during the journey, where I was all smiles:

"I didn't expect for it to feel this good, for it to be this way. My body could feel this way in daily life."

"I notice that I don't feel lonely right now. All of the outward distractions pull me away. I can't feel this way when I'm always focused outward."

"I've always been disappointed about the studies of baseline happiness, that you can't make yourself happier. But I am realizing now that I *am* happier as a baseline—I am euphoric. It just wasn't shining through."

People talk about the ineffability of psychedelic experiences—it is impossible to describe the peace and love and bliss I experienced during this journey. But I knew that this was my destined state. If I can let go of what stands in the way, this is who I am and how I'm meant to experience life.

After the guided journey, there is a time period where you integrate what you learned into your daily life. There may be some immediate takeaways, but so much of these psychedelic experiences settles in through our interactions with the world in the days and weeks that follow. I had several integration sessions with my guide, I meditated and journaled, and I participated in some community integration groups.

At times when I meditated during integration, I found my way to this blissful state again. And when I looked in the mirror, I saw myself differently. I could look deeply into my eyes and see who I really was, who I have always been. MDMA let me bask in my loving essence, in my wholeness. I am not, in fact, broken from my trauma. I am not doomed because I missed out on a mother's love during this lifetime. A mother's love is simply an arrow that points to the love within us. That I didn't have that arrow just meant that I had to find my own way to my love, combing the darkness. And finding my way to my love in the darkness has heightened my experience, sharpened my senses as I have gotten to know its texture, its shape, its depth, its power.

Cleaning the Muck

A month after my first MDMA journey, we decided to move on to psilocybin. For real this time. Psilocybin is a halluci- nogenic compound found in over two hundred species of mushrooms, referred to as *magic mushrooms*. Psilocybin's effects include an altered sense of time and space and any of a wide range of emotions, from euphoria and peacefulness to fear and paranoia. Users may report an experience of ego dissolution or ego death, losing one's sense of self, which can lead to an enhanced sense of connectedness.

My intention for this journey was to remove any internal barriers generating my loneliness, making it harder to find "my people." After my blissful experience with MDMA, I knew this experience would be different, but I trusted it would be beautiful in other ways. Borrowing from what I had heard about others' experiences, maybe I'd be an eagle flying in the sky or, through rainbow light, see that we are all one!

Nope.

I was immediately pulled into the underworld, where smirking gremlins were dancing with my dead mother's teeth. "There's more work to do," they barked.

I tried to negotiate with them—*But I've done so much work! For years! I need the reward!*

"You have your son" was the matter-of-fact response.

In contrast to my MDMA journey, where I was a chatterbox to my guide about all the beauty in me and in the world, I could barely speak during this journey. When I went to open my mouth, something would pull me under again.

The colors were muted. There was so much about death. The mushrooms said, "Look at it! Don't look away!" The message was a common one: In order to be reborn, things have to die. I faced this with great sadness. My spiritual death was already underway, having let go of so much in my life, but I mourned for all of those I knew who were clinging to their lives with such desperation. They will have to go through that death, too, to be reborn.

As I came down from the medicine and reentered my body, I felt like I had been hit by a truck. It was so much more painful than I expected. I ate a little food and slowly started to walk around the property. I sat down and tried to get some grounding by touching the grass, feeling the earth. I pet the horses. What I craved more than anything, though, was to see my son. As soon as I was cleared, I traveled back to Portland, picked him up from his dad's, and held him tight.

In the integration of this journey, I accepted that the mushrooms were just showing me what was there. I had more to face, more grief to process to show up differently in the world. So I hopped to, intentionally going toward the grief whenever I had space to do so. And every time I did, it was like cleaning muck off the windows—more light would shine through.

When my son was a baby, I'd take him out for walks in the neighborhood in a baby carrier. I was assured by others that he'd conk out when nestled against my chest like this, but he never did. Instead, he would crane his head this way and that, taking in with wide eyes the world around. After my psilocybin journey, I got a taste for what his experience might have been. It was as if the trees came alive to me. I would walk down the street and halt in front of a tree that surely I had walked by hundreds of times before. But now I *saw* it. I'd marvel, *Where have you been?*

My guide reminded me that the trees hadn't changed, I had. The rewiring of my brain—from the psychedelics and subsequent grief work—let me see things I couldn't before. It was like going from black and white to color, from two dimensions to three. I still walk around our neighborhood, wide-eyed, stunned by the intricate patterns of the branches, the geometric shadows cast by the leaves on the sidewalk below, the deepest blues of the lacecap hydrangeas, the playfulness of the tall foxgloves, the splendor of the vibrant, voluptuous dahlias. The world is so much more beautiful than I knew.

I always loved the popularized acronym AFGO—"another fucking growth opportunity." It brings lightness and humor to our common experience of constantly feeling challenged, of having yet another thing to learn on our path to self-love and self-discovery. We want to "get there," to be done with the work, because we want the pain to stop. But we know that is not an option, that resisting the learning will only bring more pain, and we must continue to work through these obstacles as they arise. It is exhausting!

When the mushrooms told me that there was more to do, I was frustrated but accepted the reality—always more work ahead. Like another wave hitting, here we go again, can I stay afloat? Now I wonder if it was my lens that processed the mushrooms' message in that way. If I see everything as something to endure, as a lesson to learn, I will hear it as "more work to do." But once I realize that with every wave of grief comes such goodness, I can understand it instead as "more beauty to uncover"—staggering, unimaginable beauty.

A Tapestry of Letting Go

I went on to have another painful psilocybin journey, so my guide offered that I might try a different medicine. Some people are mushroom people, and others find medicines like Ayahuasca to be more tolerable.

Ayahuasca is a psychoactive beverage that originates from the Amazon, typically made from two Amazonian plants. The first is *Psychotria viridis*, which contains the hallucinogenic substance N,N-Dimethyltryptamine (DMT). But DMT is not orally active due to the inactivation by monoamine oxidase (MAO) in the human gut and liver. It becomes orally active when administered with the second plant, *Banisteriopsis caapi*, which contains MAO inhibitors. Ayahuasca has been used for thousands of years by indigenous cultures and shamans for physical, mental, and spiritual healing.

Ayahuasca was more intimidating to me because of the purging element, perhaps most experienced through vomiting, but it can also be experienced through diarrhea, crying, laughter, yawning, shaking. I also was concerned about the group setting. In contrast to my MDMA and psilocybin journeys with just me and a guide, in Ayahuasca the number of people sitting for the ceremony outnumber the Ayahuasqueros, or healers, leading the ceremony. Would I get the attention I needed? Could they safely attend to everyone's experience if the ratio were not one-to-one?

But, as I always do, I went with my gut. I felt comfortable after talking with the Ayahuasquero—her energy was clean, and she knew her shit. As for the purging, having endured such painful psilocybin journeys, I knew I could handle whatever was to come—and that the pain was dwarfed by the insights and growth I had been taking away from the medicines. So I signed up for an Ayahuasca ceremony four months after my first psilocybin journey.

That first Ayahuasca ceremony began a relationship with the medicine, also referred to as "Mother Aya." I have now participated in several ceremonies, and each time feels like a continuing, connected conversation with Mother Aya. Every time she weaves another thread, helping me release that which doesn't serve.

During my first ceremony, Mother Aya told me I could set down tremendous sadness I had been feeling before the ceremony—it was old sadness. After the ceremony, it was gone. She guided me to take space in specific relationships that were not serving me. She told me that I had to let go of fear if I truly wanted to choose joy in my life. When a loved one came to mind, I thought, *I should send them healing energy*. Mother Aya said, "No, keep that for yourself." Over and over she had me set things down, let things go, pull my energy back to me.

Sometimes we have explicit conversations like this. Other times I grieve for hours, crying for the loss of my mother, of my marriage. More letting go. Still other times, Mother Aya is working in my body, and I have no conscious understanding of what is happening. I'll throw up violently, over and over, clearing things out without any clue of the what or why. I'll see classic psychedelic hallucinations—geometric landscapes shifting in and out. I'll feel her in my back, then down in my legs, and now back to my stomach. My body will disappear, leaving only breath, traveling backward and forward, backward and forward, backward and forward.

Whatever the variation, by the end, Mother Aya will deliver me in one piece and profoundly grateful for such a massive experience. Even if I can't yet piece together what that experience was.

I am a very logical, A-leads-to-B-leads-to-C person, and that is just not how integration works the bulk of the time. After a journey, I'll furiously jot down any immediate insights for fear that I'll lose them with the passage of time. But most of these journeys have taken me out of my conscious thinking, rewiring things without my ability to understand. As I go about my life in the days and weeks following the journey, things simply click in a way they didn't before.

In the week after my sixth Ayahuasca ceremony, I was out working in my yard. It was springtime, and my vine maples were in need of their annual trimming. I trimmed the new growth low on the trees, allowing them to focus their energy on growing taller rather than wider. I also trimmed offshoots that were pointed downward, and when I'd clip one of these offshoots, the rest of the branch would pop up with its newfound lightness.

Going into this ceremony, I had asked Mother Aya to remove the blocks that are keeping me from stepping into the person I'm meant to become. As I was clipping these branches, I started to understand that every decision I make is one that lets me grow upward or one that weighs me down. It's not that I have to be perfect. But I can choose, as I'd like, to move toward things that help me grow in that moment or not.

When I get stuck in a recurring thought pattern, I now envision cutting loose that offshoot and, in the quiet, find myself lighter, peaceful, clear. When I feel drained after spending time with others, I'll remain curious about which patterns I can release so that I can find more aliveness. And I'll give myself permission to retreat in order to care for my proverbial tree—taking time to rest, to better care for my body, to spend time with my son, to finish projects at home, to focus on my writing.

In the integration after this journey, I had a new, deeply embodied framework that made it so much clearer: Is this decision serving me and who I want to become?

Risky Parenting

On a surface level, it can feel surprising that I have used psychedelics when my trauma stems from my mother's use of drugs. Of course, the healing properties of psychedelics are widely known and could have helped treat my mom's depression and addiction if she had access to those resources. But even as I have used psychedelics to help me find healing, I have been scared of the instability they introduce.

After my first psilocybin journey, I knew my life was going to change monumentally. I had already decided to divorce, but the rest of my life was going to turn over as well—I just didn't know how it would play out. So my guide and I talked about keeping scaffolding in place, not making any big moves. My son and I would stay in our house for now. I wouldn't go recklessly tearing apart all of my relationships or shutting down my business. Things would unfold organically.

But the organic unfolding of a spiritual awakening is not smooth or predictable. Crises come when they come, grief doesn't give notice. And each time a wave would come, I felt saddened, fearful, and guilty—being immersed in grief meant I couldn't be fully present with my son. Even so, I'd press on, knowing deep down that these temporary periods of being less present were in service to the larger picture: bringing healing to our family and giving my son the best chance for a love-filled, joyful life.

When I became pregnant with my son, a part of me came back to life. For a long time, I wasn't sure I even wanted kids—since I felt like a burden as a child, I didn't understand why I'd want that for myself. But my co-parent was very eager to be a father, and I warmed up to it given he would carry much of the load. Amidst several miscarriages, my son is my miracle baby, though it felt like I was growing the devil within, with the debilitating nausea, fiery reflux, and his never-ending goddamn hiccups. Being pregnant led me to do things I'd never contemplated, like parking on the side of the road and eating a blackberry pie directly out of the tin—pie-contest style—after driving around forever trying to find something I could stomach.

It also made me love with abandon, waking up a part of me that had been deeply asleep since the loss of my mom. I cared more profoundly for this mysterious, hiccupping devil than I remembered ever caring for anything or anyone. And of course this love only grew as I got to know this munchkin, who to this day erupts into hiccups with every fit of laughter.

Psychedelics have augmented my experience as a mother in ways that I could not have imagined. My son offers me a glimpse into the magical world that exists beyond what I have known in my human experience, and having more of the curtain pulled back only enhances my ability to see his magic. As my guide predicted, my love for him has intensified and clarified, and he senses this. His eyes light up when he is seen, and he becomes more engaging, more charming, more playful, more hilarious. Then my love for him grows, and then he brings more magic and then more love and then more magic.

But there are a handful of times when I have thought, *Oh, Alexis, what have you done?*

———

I did my last psilocybin journey by myself in my living room at home, with my guide on call in case I needed her. I was euphoric at times and deeply sad at other times. I sobbed about feeling so restricted in my life when I needed to be doing more, to shine more. I needed to sing. To play the drums. To move my body. At the end of the journey, the mushrooms asked me if I wanted to see something dark. Knowing the darkness has always led me to more light, I said, *Sure*.

"Turn off the music," they said.

Okay.

When all was quiet, the mushrooms said, "You don't want to live."

Silence.

Is there more? Is that it?

Silence.

I was lying there on the couch in complete silence and stillness. I felt like a corpse. This was too much. I can't see that. I have a child, and I can't not want to live. I have to want to live. *Please tell me there's more, that there's an offsetting, positive truth here.*

Silence.

A phone call from my guide interrupted my panic and immediately helped me see that this was from my lineage— my grandfather, who died by suicide, and my mother, who died from complications with addiction and depression. This was what I was working so hard to heal. I wasn't clear if the insight offered by the mushrooms was my emotion or if it was showing me that I was storing my mother's or my grandfather's emotion in my body. In *It Didn't Start with You*, clinical psychologist Mark Wolynn explains how our parents' and grandparents' traumas can be stored in our DNA and can be felt as if they are our own, can impact our lives as if we had experienced the traumatic events firsthand.

I realized it didn't matter whose it was—in the darkness, it impacted my life. In the light, I could heal it, diffuse it, release it.

Knowing this emotion was in my body emboldened my dedication to making sure I was fed. Like a plant not getting enough nutrients, we simply can't keep going if we aren't being fed—fed by love, nurturing, celebration, inspiration. What I don't know is whether the mechanical efforts I made to give myself more nutrients made a difference or whether the insight simply opened up my ability to receive more of the nutrients that were already there. Rumi says that beauty is for the one who sees. Did acknowledging this emotion let me become one who can see?

Before, this truth was there in the shadow, in the unconscious. And avoiding it didn't negate it, it only made it more powerful. By acknowledging it and welcoming it, I diffused it.

The hard doesn't stay. The darkness doesn't stay. Once felt fully, it heals.

———

In my efforts to wake up, to un-numb, I have had these moments where I've felt terrified, deeply saddened, or untethered, and I think of that as a risk to my son. I don't want to ever risk my ability to show up for him. I don't want a tragic repeat of what happened to me.

But this fear has shifted in my mind. I am willing to brave these dark, scary places to carve out a different trajectory for our family. And the fact that I have my son lets me brave these places.

There is a picture of us gazing into each other's eyes when he was a very young baby. I have the sense that when

I became pregnant, when my son was born, he was saying to me, "I'm here!" Picking up the baton, ready to support me as I embarked on this journey. We are in this lineage healing together. I am doing the hard work for him, and he is giving me the fuel I need—joy and love and grounding—to keep going.

So Many Parts

It wasn't until my co-parent and I initially went to couples counseling that I even considered individual therapy, at the suggestion of our therapist. I didn't know that my childhood was traumatic. I just knew I was sad at times about my mom dying.

During my first individual therapy session, sitting on a purple couch in a lavender room on the twelfth floor of a downtown Portland high-rise, I explained to my therapist that I had been trained in nonviolent communication and was very in touch with my feelings and needs. She kindly and respectfully listened but, over time, gently guided me to be more open to what I had gone through and how that affected me. She introduced me to the idea that there was a "little Alexis" within me that needed compassion and care for her feelings—compassion and care that she didn't receive as a child.

Since I discounted my trauma as not meaningful, I had a hard time connecting with this little Alexis. What's the big deal? And I found relating to myself in this way—as both an adult and a child version of me—to be awkward and uncomfortable. But I gave it a try. I'd imagine the sadness another child would feel if they lost their mom, put my hand on my heart, and honor the feeling of sadness felt by little Alexis. Tending to myself with gentle touch and compassion seemed to soften something in me. And over time, this exchange between adult Alexis and little Alexis became easier, more trusting. I started to understand and feel understood for the depth of pain I experienced as a kid.

Internal Family Systems, also known as *parts work*, is a psychotherapy framework developed by Dr. Richard Schwartz. I delved more deeply into parts work with my psychedelic guide and *Healing the Fragmented Selves of Trauma Survivors* by Janina Fisher. My basic understanding is that when we experience a trauma—something that is beyond our capacity to process—a part of ourselves gets frozen at that time. This part can get triggered by events that lead it to believe that it is, in fact, back in the traumatizing event.

When someone is late by even just a few minutes, a part of me might panic due to my childhood abandonment, believing 100 percent that I am being abandoned again and that bad shit is about to go down. The person I loved most in the world was supposed to go away for only three weeks, and she never came home. My outsized reaction to someone being late is a part that is afraid that this unexpected change in plans foretells devastating loss.

If you are unaware of these parts, you blend with them and can't see anything but that story—that you are unsafe, back in the trauma, with no way out. The hope is to be able to watch these emotions, keeping your higher self in charge so you can stay present and help these parts begin to heal.

While doing this work, what I discovered was—dear god—there is not just *one* little Alexis, there is a whole crew! There is in utero Alexis and newborn Alexis and Alexis at many different ages. Each is stuck in time from their specific trauma, which means that each one has different needs, often competing—it is like a boardroom of kids, and whoever yells the loudest wins. The other Alexises sit there while I care for the "winner," annoyed that they have not gotten the attention they want but primed to scream the loudest next.

When my co-parent moved out of the house, I had a part scared to be alone in the house, a part who felt she lost herself when others weren't around, a part who was terrified my co-parent's leaving means he might die like my mom did, a part who was just sad all the time, a part who desperately wanted to keep moving forward on this growth path after feeling stagnant for so long. I was exhausted by what felt like a constant need for re-parenting. But I would try to tend to these parts both emotionally—honor their feelings—and physically—*Do you want to go for a walk, do you want to call a friend, can I get you something to eat?* Slowly, they started feeling cared for and were triggered less frequently.

And—they needed more. During a period of deep sadness, I became overwhelmed. So overwhelmed, in fact, that I threw a temper tantrum on my kitchen floor. I literally yelled out loud at the universe, "I need a sign that I'm not alone! ANYTHING! Could be that as I walk by the coffee shop someone hands me a FREE CUPCAKE! Or as I walk by the pet food store someone hands me a FREE PUPPY!" I went for a walk to give the universe a chance to show its support.

But I returned home from my walk with zero cupcakes and zero puppies, deflated and exhausted. So I reached out to my guide, who helped me realize I needed to take a break from the sadness. I was blending with the sadness—it was actually a part that needed me to manage her exposure to her triggers. Like turning off a movie that is more advanced than your child can handle, I had to tell that part, for example, *No, you can't read that text exchange again right now*. The part needed a break, and it was my parental responsibility to set boundaries for her. This boundary-setting is a huge shift. Before, my parts were feeling loved and understood and tended to, but no one was in charge. Now they can relax, knowing that Mom is on it.

Obviously there are not actual small children within my body. It is stuck energy, wiring in my brain that got off-course from my trauma. But characterizing that stuck energy as innocent children lets me love that energy the way I know to love as a human. And loving that energy moves it, disrupting my ingrained circuitry to allow for new, more expansive circuits to form.

Managing these parts has made me a better mom to my son too. In parenting my parts, I'm learning how to help my kiddo when he feels stuck with the Rolodex of "What do you need right now?" offerings. And I'm getting better at getting ahead of my younger parts so they are not the ones interacting with my son—my adult self is.

Once, after school, my son was struggling during a miserable bike ride home, drenched after a run-in with a puddle and unrelenting rain. As he pedaled and cried, I empathized with how terrible this must feel. Several minutes in, I noticed feeling aggravated, as one of my parts started feeling stressed about not being able to resolve my son's distress. There are times when this part proceeds unchecked, and my dysregulation joins my son's dysregulation for a big dysregulation party. This time, however, I quickly and firmly said, *No.* to the part. And the aggravation disappeared. She just needed to know it wasn't hers to solve, and she immediately felt relieved.

Of course, I can't always get there before my part is off to the races. One day I felt overwhelmed by the preparations for a big trip my then six-year-old son and I were about to take. I had taken a break from the preparations to go swimming with my son, but my attention span was short as the seemingly endless to-dos ran through my brain. When my son wanted me to watch him do a trick in the pool or splashed me, I became irritated. I could observe this overwhelm and irritation instead of unconsciously acting from it, and I tried to let him in on my overwhelm and my plans to manage it. Frolicking around in the pool, he was shockingly uninterested! While I could observe the overwhelm and irritation some, his flippant response to me triggered further irritation, and some seeped out in his direction.

When we got out of the pool for a snack, I apologized and started to explain what was going on with me. Wrapped in a towel and mouth full of soft pretzel, he cut me off, saying, "I know, Little Mommy is having a hard time."

I sat stunned, relieved, and grinning from ear to ear. From our prior conversations, he knew that when I did not act in my typical loving, present way, it was not about him—it was a young part of me who remained stuck in the trauma, still in need of healing. Because I had interpreted all of the disconnection in my childhood as being about me, I have been very intentional about taking responsibility and giving space for my son's emotions after I've been dysregulated. And I'm thrilled that he knows what it means to be dysregulated so that he can both have compassion for others who are in that experience and not take on their emotions as his responsibility. It's really just helping him see what is real—our loving connection—and what is a distortion—my trauma response.

———

During my first psilocybin journey, the mushrooms unapologetically told me that I had more work to do, and when I pleaded with them for a reward, they said, "You have your son." I thought, *Yeah, I should be grateful.* But that *should* was a reflection of a block—I was not able to fully receive him as a gift to me for some reason. As a parent, I had internalized that I am supposed to be there for my kid, not to need something from him. Especially with a mother who struggled with addiction, I wouldn't dare put my needs on my kid. But we are here to receive and be received! For me to not look to my child for joy, to not look to my child for love, means I am not accepting the gifts that he is here to give.

And I have discovered that not all parts work is parental in the sense of giving to that little kiddo within. One time I noticed that I felt "off" and wondered if there were parts I had been unaware of that needed some love. So I put on some music and went on a walk, imagining holding baby Alexis to my chest to comfort her. Instead, I was blown away, filled with extraordinary light and love from this little one. What she needed was not tending or help but to be received.

In sorting through memorabilia from my younger years, I have found multiple notes from different loved ones with the phrase, "I do love you." As if there was some internal struggle before coming to that conclusion. While friends, teachers, and strangers would flock to me, sharing their love and adoration, for these loved ones there was a block. They couldn't take in my gifts, couldn't find sustenance in my warmth, my playfulness, my loving nature.

But now I get to provide the forum for my precious parts who are so eager to share what they couldn't those many years ago. I am filled by my joyfulness and my creativity. And increasingly I find my way to people whose eyes light up when I share my gifts with them.

Coping Messengers

While my older sisters were in summer camp, I kicked off my summer days with *The Price Is Right*. I plopped onto my stomach in front of the TV with snacks at hand. I'd empty out a box of Lucky Charms and separate the *healthy* brown pieces from the marshmallows so I could get right to the good stuff. We had a very sweet housekeeper named Bernie who would make me Kraft Mac & Cheese or SpaghettiOs for lunch. As we moved into the soap opera segment of the day—*The Young and the Restless* and *Days of Our Lives*—the snack rotation continued as well. I'd reach for a Little Debbie snack from the shallow drawer beneath the oven, or I'd get out the Oreos and a knife and begin my operation of expanding a single Oreo to include the icing of ten Oreos.

To make up for the excitement, inspiration, and intimacy I was missing, I ate. To avoid feeling the intense loneliness and stress of my isolation, I ate.

And this continued into adulthood as I perpetuated my childhood patterns of neglect. My default was always to help others without checking in about my own needs first. I would take a stressful call from a struggling family member only to miss my exercise class. I would show up for others in lieu of billing hours. At some point, I realized that every time I impulsively picked up the phone and took ownership over my loved ones' problems, I was neglecting myself and I'd have to compensate for that neglect by eating. Every time I took on too much work for clients who had urgent deadlines, I'd reach for a Coke, some ice cream, something delicious to push through and lessen the feeling of stress.

When I started relinquishing that illusion of responsibility, I stopped reaching for the food. When I learned to care for myself, I stopped reaching for the food. I just didn't need it like before.

Cravings are messengers that we're missing something. We are going to keep reaching for the food, wine, screens, [fill in the blank] until we learn what we need and start providing that. I still indulge in cravings before checking in. But I am learning that when I have a strong craving for sugar, it's a part of me saying, *I need something I'm not getting.* If I can slow myself down, I can say, *Oh, hi there, little one. How can I care for you right now?*

You're feeling stressed about this work deadline? You're feeling sad that I accepted this short deadline before checking in about what you need? That makes so much sense—I am really sorry, and I'll see what I can do to adjust. You are the most important. Part feels loved, held, craving goes away.

You're really wanting that ice cream right now because you are scared we won't get to have it again? I understand. Let me promise you this—I will drive all the way over to this ice cream shop anytime you want. Part feels relieved, perceiving abundance instead of lack, doesn't need ice cream anymore.

When I do indulge before slowing down, I have an icky feeling after. I used to understand this as guilt or shame—thinking that I'm not strong enough or that I did a "bad" thing by indulging and will feel the physical ramifications of it. But cravings are just another version of parts work. A part of us is asking for love and care—and also offering themselves to us. Cravings offer us a chance to discover something new about ourselves that will blow our minds and fill our hearts. And when I unconsciously reach for the sugar, I've missed it. For now.

—

My desire for sugar is not the only messenger that there is a part of me needing to be seen—I cope in all sorts of ways, but most of the time I don't even realize I'm coping, that I'm trying to avoid pain.

There are times when I do not like to be in my house alone, and I have to get out in nature. I can experience anxiety about being in a hotel room without outdoor access. I can take forever to book a vacation home as I try to get a sense for whether I'll feel comfortable. When my co-parent and I were separated, I rented an Airbnb in San Francisco for a few days while on a work trip, and feeling that sad and alone in a strange apartment felt almost unbearable. So it's not as much about comfort as what feels like survival. If I am in a fragile emotional state, being isolated indoors can be terrifying for me.

I grew up in a lovely 4,000-square foot home on 1.5 acres in Northeast Texas. But no one knew what was going on inside. The absence. The silence. The loneliness. The neglect. I was stuck in this beautiful prison where no one knew to come rescue me. I don't remember feeling pain around this—maybe boredom as I watched a billion hours of TV, but not pain. And now I know it's because it was too much for me, and I cut off the connection to the pain.

My fear around being sad and alone indoors has been trying to get my attention so that I could heal, so that I could bring back this part of me that has been lost. Because you can't shut down the pain and keep the good—numbing is a package deal. But I have avoided feeling this pain by coping. And my coping mechanisms are benign and socially acceptable, so I did not feel challenged to look deeper. I want to be outdoors—who doesn't? Our souls are filled by the beauty of Mother Nature. I want to go to a coffee shop to work instead of being at home—who wouldn't? Enjoying a change of scenery, the fun music and energy, is totally understandable. And occasionally watching a show at night and enjoying something snacky or sweet is completely normal.

During a phase of drawing daily tarot cards, I drew the Devil card multiple times, which suggests, among other things, looking at your addictions. I was annoyed. I have a pretty clean diet—a far cry from my college diet of pizza and fudge—so give me a break. My cravings have subsided substantially since I've started taking better care of myself in relationship with others. I don't have to be perfect! But goddammit, the cards were right. Underneath these remaining, though lessened, cravings and other coping mechanisms was a mound of pain I was avoiding.

As this part of me started waking up, it felt like more than I could handle. I began to press just a little, considering dropping some of my coping strategies—perhaps booking a vacation home where the bedroom was tucked in the back of the home, lacking light or visible connection to the outside world. The emotions that surfaced in response were massive. Sitting on my living room floor, arms wrapped tightly around myself, I shook in terror. I wailed, screamed with pain about being so alone and unsupported.

It can be so easy to downplay what we went through as children precisely because of our body's ability to dissociate. It can't have been that bad because we don't remember it being that bad. But when I am convulsing on the floor from the pain of being alone in a building, I can no longer downplay what I went through as trivial. Adding in the complexity of intergenerational trauma that might be stored in our bodies and—if it's your jam—the potential for pain that we're carrying from past lifetimes, the origin doesn't really matter. It matters that it is trying to get our attention so we may release it and find more peace, more joy, more safety, more beauty.

And our cravings and coping mechanisms are our little messengers telling us, *Psst! There's something to see here!*

Along my journey, therapists told me that my coping was healthy. My take? Kinda sorta. Ultimately, I don't want to cope. I want to harvest all of the treasures that are waiting for me. If I had kept coping on all these fronts, I wouldn't have woken up the parts of me that have led me to so much love and joy and creativity. But we can only do what we can do when we can do it. So coping until I am ready for that next level is what I'm going to do. Sometimes I am ready in a graceful, peaceful, intentional manner. And sometimes, when part of my life threatens to fall apart, I'm like, *Fuck, okay, okay, I'll look at it!*

About cravings, Rumi says,

> Your desire for the illusory is a wing, by means of which a seeker might ascend to Reality. When you have indulged a lust, your wing drops off; you become lame and that fantasy flees. Preserve the wing and don't indulge such lust, so that the wing of desire may bear you to Paradise. People fancy they are enjoying themselves, but they are really tearing out their wings for the sake of an illusion.

When I first read this, standing in my kitchen, I remarked to myself, *How profound.* And then I walked across the room and opened a bag of chips that I wasn't hungry for.

We'll get there.

Double Take

Before each of my psychedelic journeys, my guide would lead me through a tarot or oracle card pull. One time I pulled a card labeled "Emotions," which said I should pay attention to mine. *Okay, Captain Obvious*, we both thought. Of course I pay attention to my emotions—it's what I do all the livelong day. But, turns out, as with everything, there were layers and layers that I had not yet become conscious of. Like all the times I felt something and then told myself not to. At an intersection when another driver acted aggressively, I would have an initial frustrated reaction and then quickly tell myself to have compassion. No one hurts unless they are themselves hurt, so I should not be offended.

And this kind of messaging—to ignore, reject, suppress, repress our feelings—is pervasive. You shouldn't be angry, look at the bright side, others have it worse. Maybe a fairer statement would be that we don't want to get stuck in our emotions. But the feelings themselves carry important messages for us. Every feeling, every sensation that we have is something that is trying to get our attention. This too-obvious card helped me to slow down. I get to feel! There's more to harvest in this emotion. Don't throw it away!

My favorite discovery amidst this new curiosity is seeing jealousy and longings differently. In my experience, jealously had a bad rap—from the tenth commandment to an encouragement to find gratitude for what you have instead of wanting something else. But when I am jealous of someone, it's because I see something in them that is in me, something from which I have lost connection. The jealousy is an arrow pointing to something hidden inside of me that is ready to come out. Instead of rejecting the jealousy, can I be curious and follow that string?

I took a free barre class at a local athletic wear store when I was thirty years old. I had not been exercising much, really since high school, and I found it so fun to feel challenged athletically again after all these years. My calves were so sore after that first mini class that each time I stood up, I involuntarily blurted out, "Fuck!" As painful as it was, I loved this feeling of soreness, giving me a glimpse of the power I had to make a difference in my life. I decided to try out a full class in the studio in Portland. The practice in this barre studio is to help students individually adjust their positioning to make sure they are doing each exercise safely and most effectively. During my first class, a woman named Amanda got called on over and over—"Amanda, raise your heels higher." "Amanda, engage your core." "Amanda, align your shoulders directly above your hips." In the last few minutes of class, I cracked up when I realized the instructor just had my name wrong—*I am Amanda!*

I always desired more community. I felt so alone my whole life. And I'd feel jealous of others who seemed to have found community. I'd see women working out together on the street or in someone's driveway and feel saddened. Why don't I have that kind of luck? Why don't I live on the street with the woman who teaches exercise? I'd accept my loneliness as my fate in this lifetime. I'd give myself compassion for the loneliness, for the sadness, and I'd remain there.

During the pandemic, I led myself through daily barre workouts. With ten years of barre classes under my belt, I had the equation down. And I started wondering about inviting other moms on my street to come join me on my porch or in my driveway. It was outside of my comfort zone to do this for a few reasons. Most significantly, I was conditioned to thinking that I didn't have anything attractive to offer, that people didn't want to be friends with me. Related, I assumed that if people did want to hang with me, they would have reached out before, so I was headed into known defeat. Another obstacle was that I was used to basically never talking. It was a big step up for me to count out loud and lead people through exercises. And I had to get my act together a little—between having enough weights for people, putting together playlists, and having a routine ready.

Despite these challenges, I was determined to start doing things differently in my life. I had always solved for what I knew I could do, for what would bring praise. But what did that get me? My life was declared a tragedy by the voice in the woods, and my marriage was over. Screw that, I was ready to find out what I was made of. Bring on the stretch experiences.

Around the time my co-parent moved out, I emailed five women, and before the *woosh* sound even finished on the email exiting my outbox, I regretted it. *How embarrassing, what was I thinking, no one is going to say yes.* And then one accepted. *Oh thank god. But no one else is going to join, and this will be such a failure,* I assured myself. And then another, and then all of them. And porch barre was born.

Turns out I did live on the street with the woman who teaches exercise—I just didn't realize it was me! Because I accepted my loneliness and sadness as my destined state, I missed out on these other messages about the gifts I had to contribute, about my power to create community, about how rewarding it can be to take a risk, to step outside my comfort zone.

Now, when I notice something I want, when I feel my heart lift, I say to myself, *Ah, that's coming.* Instead of focusing on the sadness of not having what I want and trying to find healing for that sadness, I see the longing as foreshadowing what is to come. Then I become fed by the longing, grateful for what is to be. And with that grateful, loving energy, I invite that outcome into my life.

Divine Fishnets

I always wanted to take dance class when I was little, but my mom signed me up for a ballet class that was too young for me, and I never took dance again. When I was in high school, I had a blast dancing as a cheerleader. But mostly I just watched with great admiration and jealousy as my friends took dance classes and danced competitively, begging them to teach me their routines. In *Calling in "The One,"* Katherine Woodward Thomas encourages you to take a risk to express more of your authentic self, to let part of you that has been hidden come into view. Around the same time I started porch barre, I signed up for an adult beginner ballet class. And I bought myself the leotard, the skirt, the tights, the shoes. It was so healing to do this for myself after wishing it had been done for me as a child. I enjoyed watching myself doing these graceful ballerina movements to classical music.

And then I found a badass modern burlesque-style dance class and chucked my leotard and ballet shoes for some heeled boots and knee pads. Though I didn't start out so bold! For my first class, surrounded by women in fishnets and heels, I nervously hid in the back, barefoot in an athletic tank and yoga pants. The talented and engaging instructor began teaching us eight counts and then turned on the music: Bishop Briggs's version of "Never Tear Us Apart," featured in the Fifty Shades of Grey movie series. In some ways, I was completely out of my element, barely keeping up as others expertly and seductively moved their hips and whipped their heads around. In other ways, I had never felt so beautiful and alive—well, at least not in a very long time.

When I was maybe six years old, I remember pacing the mirrored living room of my aunt's small condo on Marco Island, Florida. I was wearing a new purple one-piece swim-suit edged with yellow ruffles and had an unapologetic pro-truding belly at that time. I could not get enough! I was blown away by my beauty in this new suit, and the mirrored wall gave me the chance to take in the view as I walked back and forth, admiring myself from every angle. I can't remember which family member discovered me mid-promenade, but the tale born from that scene was a gentle mocking of my childish self-absorption and adoration. Under the laughter, I internalized that my admiring my body was embarrassing and shameful.

I took a few decades off, but I'm at it again. I love watching videos of myself dancing my burlesque routines. I love being in the front row at my dance studio so I can watch my body move. During one class we danced to Nessa Barrett's "madhouse," wearing knee pads and heels and using a chair as our prop. Whipping my hair around, hiking my leg up on the chair, moving with such a commanding energy—I felt incredible. After the class, an instructor came up to me to tell me how captivating I was in the dance. I was so flattered by her comment. And I was also like, *I know, right?* I am captivated. I cannot believe this is me.

Turns out, my admiration for my body was not and is not a distortion. What I saw as a young girl and lost the ability to see until more recently was the divine in me. And to appreciate this beautiful human body we inhabit—the lines, the curves, the shapes, the colors—that can move in such elegant, stirring ways. Adorned by textile creations of artists that help us reveal more of who we are within.

I sometimes think of Uncle Rico in the movie *Napolean Dynamite*. How he longed for his glory days and was stuck there—and is a pitiable character because of it. But who of us isn't Uncle Rico? We hide it better, we've accepted defeat more readily. But don't we all long for something more, something bigger for ourselves and our lives? And we've been taught to shut that down. As I have begun to pursue my longings, my life is more, my life is bigger, I have come alive. I still have the doubts and the fears and the self-consciousness—it will be a lifetime of work to welcome, honor, and release those emotions. But when the music starts playing and it is time to dance, I say to myself, *I am god*, and I kick ass.

Knock Knock

As I remember it, there was an armchair in the corner of my parents' bedroom where my two older sisters and I received big news I could not understand. When I was eleven, this is where I learned that my mom was sick and would be going away to rehab for three weeks. And eighteen months later, as we were getting ready for her funeral, my father told us of a rumor circulating that my mom had another child. Hearing it framed that way, I assumed that meant it was not true. Five years later, it popped into my head to ask my dad if it was true—and he said it was.

My mother's family was a lovely, talented, warm family, adored by their community. My mother competed in the Miss Teen USA competition, and she was named a "Baylor

Beauty" in a pageant at Baylor University in Waco, Texas. My aunt was crowned homecoming queen while at Baylor. So it threatened to be a terrible mark on the family when my mom got pregnant while at university. She was sent away to have the baby and give her up for adoption, all under the ruse of helping an ailing aunt in Pennsylvania.

As all children do, I pieced together stories about what happened to me as a child to help me cope. My mother couldn't be the issue—I needed her to be reliable and loving and perfect—so it had to be me. I wasn't deserving or important or lovable. I was too much, a burden. And this gave me a sense of control. If I can show up in a different way, I can be deserving and important and lovable and just right.

The fact that my mother had this other child was barely a footnote to my story. My sisters and my father and I endured the shattering of our lives with my mom's departure. My half sister had her own family and their own storyline. I almost never thought of her. In my early thirties, I started hearing more about her—she was in contact with my father, with my extended family. I stumbled upon her Facebook photo. *Wow, she looks like my mom.*

A decade later during a guided psilocybin journey, my half sister, Julie, came into view. After that journey, I reached out to her to offer to talk on the phone. Julie shared with me that she and my mother had connected once. Julie had tracked her down, and my mother kindly made time for a phone call but could not offer her anything else. She had a family to protect, to care for. I had heard that my mother may have met up with Julie toward the end of her life, but

Julie said that didn't happen. She never heard from her beyond that single phone call.

My extended family had been kind and welcoming to Julie, but it was harder for my sisters and me. There was not enough of my mother to go around, so we couldn't afford to share her with Julie. Thirty years after my mother died, we are all still reeling from the loss of her. But my psilocybin journey helped me see that Julie was as much my mother's daughter as my sisters and I were. In our conversation, I called my mom "our mom," and Julie was so touched that I would include her in that description.

I shared with Julie how, even if my mom didn't meet up with her toward the end of her life, the fact that someone thought she did meant my mom was thinking of her. I offered the likelihood that my mother's depression was tied at least in part to her love for Julie, her heartache that she couldn't be with her every day. Julie is not a footnote. She has her own chapter in my mother's life, just as my sisters and I do.

———

Given my lifetime of heartbreak, I have always focused on my heart as the place where my pain is stored, where my energy is stuck. But during an Ayahuasca ceremony, Mother Aya said, "Pssst! It's down there!" She was pointing at my stomach.

One of my intentions coming into the ceremony was finding clarity around my over-protectiveness for my son, which was so draining for me. At the start of the ceremony, I was grieving how little control I had over my son's well-being. He is on his own journey during this lifetime. The grieving intensified, and I began sobbing and pleading, "Please don't take him away from me! Don't take him away from me!" And I realized my being overprotective of him was an effort to avoid the sadness of losing him. And that this sadness was not my sadness, but my mother's sadness for losing Julie. Her sadness that this precious baby she created and loved with her whole being was entirely out of her reach. She could not love her or protect her as she was meant to, and it was more than she could bear.

I carried my mother's grief in my womb. I have had multiple miscarriages, including one that involved a dramatic string of dilation and curettage (D&C) procedures to scrape the lining of my uterus—the doctors struggled to get my body to release the fetal tissue.

I realized that my body desperately clung to these babies after they died, as my mother desired to hold on to Julie. And my mother's grief was going to stay in my body until it felt witnessed.

Before this Ayahuasca ceremony, I had been curious if there really was more sadness to process. Some talk about our bodies becoming chemically addicted to certain emotions so we re-create circumstances in our lives to feed that addiction. But boy, did I have more sadness to process. I just didn't know it wasn't all mine. My mother's sadness was showing up in my life over and over again in an effort to be seen.

So I cried and cried in acknowledgment of the grief she lived with every day not to be the mother of my oldest sister. I know the work I did in the ceremony to acknowledge my mother's grief is a big step toward the healing that her pain in my body needs. There is also a spaciousness that comes with understanding that not all the pain I feel is mine. It lets me be more curious, more yielding. When I feel overprotective of my son, I can notice that and say, *Oh, that's my mom. That's not me.* And that gives space for me to feel and honor the pain but not be attached to it, to any story around it. And that lets the energy move.

But my pain is harder. The sadness I feel for the loss of my mom feels unbearable and permanent. When I stop to sit with my grief about my mom, I go into agonizing rounds of *I'll never see her again, my heart is broken forever.*

During one of my psilocybin journeys, I reunited with my mother. We were not in human form, and it lacked the emotion that would have accompanied a human reconciliation—it was simply being together in truth. I learned that my mom left me to become compost. She left so that she could go back into the ground and become the nutrients that I needed, so that I could grow into who I'm meant to be.

I'm not attached to a concrete understanding here, but it did give some space around the loss of my mom, that perhaps it wasn't as I have always held it—as a pointless, irreparable, forever tragedy. Perhaps a larger, exquisite design is at play.

I can begin to see that part of the learning from my Ayahuasca ceremony is to take pointers from the intergenerational pain. My pain about the loss of my mom is not "me" either. It is a feeling based on a story I told myself about her death when I was young—a story I didn't even recognize as a story, as something I could question until now. If I can bring awareness to that story, if I can sit in the pain without attachment to the story, the energy here will start to move too.

Hindsight

My co-parent and I were standing outside my house, catching up on a few logistical items after he dropped off our son. He had cleared the huge hurdle of getting moved into his new apartment, set up beautifully for our son with a train-themed lamp, train-themed bedding, and a fantastic view of a bunch of train tracks on the other side of the Willamette River. The kid liked trains!

Next, we needed to figure out how to formally get divorced. As my co-parent went to get into his car, he said, "I guess we should find lawyers?"

I shrieked, "No! We are on the same team!"

He laughed, with a slight eyeroll, at my dramatic flair. But the truth was that I was passionately committed to making our separation as kind and supportive as possible. Over and over again, I have intentionally infused our relationship with generosity and love, and my co-parent has reciprocated at each step. Because we lack tension, our son has not once exhibited tension about the new family structure. It's a dream divorce.

So it surprised me when, nearly two years after we decided to divorce, I cried for hours during an Ayahuasca ceremony about losing my marriage. I cried about every angle of it. About wanting so desperately for our marriage to work and not getting there. About all of the ways in which I felt misunderstood, not seen by my co-parent. But maybe most about how sorry I was for all the dysfunction I brought to the relationship.

We struggled with so many issues that I no longer see as issues. I don't know how many hours of therapy we spent on the single seemingly insignificant topic of punctuality. On this and every other issue, there was a focus on my co-parent changing his behavior so I would no longer hurt. And now I realize that completely missed the point. I freaked out around his being late because I was abandoned over and over again by my mother. When he was late, my hypervigilance, which then morphed into frustration and ultimately panic, really had nothing to do with him. I wanted him to change his behavior so I would no longer hurt, but I was going to hurt in this same way until I was willing to face the depth of pain I experienced as a child. And we can take it one step further: It's not just that my co-parent's being late wasn't the underlying issue, it was actually a gift to me. It was a repeated opportunity for me to heal. Each time he was late and I felt pain, it was my body saying, *Let's heal this. Right now.* The triggers were gifts this whole time.

Toward the end of our marriage, I had a moment of clarity when my co-parent asked me if I could get empathy elsewhere. I knew I needed lots of it—from the painful misconnections in our marriage to the way I experienced the world around me. But I was dumbfounded. Where else would I get it if not from my life partner? What is our marriage if I cannot rely on him for that? This was a turning point in my decision to move forward with the divorce.

But after our divorce, it dawned on me one day that I do not seek empathy from others. Not that I never would, but the bulk of the time, I give that to myself. So this pivotal moment that informed my decision to leave my marriage has been turned on its head—my co-parent was right to ask me whether empathy was something I needed from him. Turns out it's not. In fact, I don't *want* empathy from others most of the time. In my all-consuming desire to know myself more and find healing, giving myself empathy and tuning in to my emotions is the key.

While in my marriage, I fantasized about feeling loved and adored. Melody Beattie's *Codependent No More* lists escape fantasies as one of the characteristics of codependency, and I was puzzled—who doesn't have fantasies about living another life? Marriage is reputationally hard and full of sacrifice and compromise, so who wouldn't wish for something easier?

But I was codependent. I constantly took responsibility for things that were not mine and demanded change of my co-parent that was not mine to demand. This tight grip robbed the relationship of the space necessary for vibrant love to grow. My codependence kept me from the very connection I so desperately desired.

Sometimes we have to try something on, find some truth, and then try something else on. And sometimes, in order to find the momentum to leave our side of the spectrum, we need to overcorrect before we can rest somewhere in the middle. In my marriage, instead of shedding the things that were not serving me, I shed the whole relationship. I do not see this as a mistake—I did not have the tools to do it differently then. And I needed the momentum to become unstuck. I took the path that I needed to take to find what I have found today.

—

I have spent countless hours wondering why my co-parent and I were together and why we didn't make it. During my first Ayahuasca ceremony, Mother Aya told me that time spent in dissociation is not wasted, it is needed rest. Could it be that my co-parent and I came together in dissociation to compress the coil spring, storing more and more energy so that we'd be ready to spring forward with huge momentum toward who we're destined to become? I was with my co-parent as a safe place to park until I was ready. I was cooking. My co-parent was a caring, protective partner for me, and I for him. The seeds were being nurtured, ready to burst through in beauty that I had not known before. Some think we make agreements prior to incarnating to help each other discover who we are and learn our desired lesson. Did my co-parent and I dock together in our spirit agreement, to stay there until our next phase?

Heck if I know. Mother Aya also said I didn't have to clean things up, that I could leave things behind. So I have had the sense that the *why* of my marriage and divorce is something I can set down now. I am left with a ton of gratitude for our love for each other and for our precious son. I am left with sadness for the parts of our relationship that were beautiful and came to an end. And I will continue to harvest the wisdom from this sadness whenever it arises.

We think of divorce as something to be avoided because it is so painful. But the pain is there, however we deal with it or however it looks. My pain with my co-parent is about my childhood. In marriage, in divorce, it is about my childhood. And as I continue to heal those wounds, the pain will lessen, and more beauty will present itself.

———

I know so many struggle with pain in their marriages, wishing for more love, more connection, more support, more something. With so much on the line, it can feel impossible to make a decision about whether to stay or go.

The relieving news to me is that there's so much to do before even getting close to a decision. And the to-do list really includes one main thing: listening to our emotions. Not pushing them down or turning them away but remaining open and curious because they have important information for us. Not accepting society's position against anger but honoring it—it's our being's way of getting in touch with how immensely strong we are. When I feel jealous, it is an arrow that points to something I am meant to have. When I feel smothered, I am taking on someone else's stuff and need better energetic boundaries. When I feel rejected, it is often about how I hold space for someone else without first considering what I want or need. When I feel uninspired, it can be that I am looking externally for something that is already within me, and when I pull my energy back to me, I find the interest and creativity I desire.

The more we get in touch with ourselves, the clearer we will be about what is right. It may be that we transform and staying is right, or it might be clear as day that it's time to go. And it might be that our transformation alights a transformation in our loved ones.

When my son gets a new piano piece, he feels intimidated by how hard it will surely be—a whole song he doesn't know. So I say, "Let's just look at the first line." Still too much. "Let's just look at the first measure." Still too much. "Let's just look at the first note. What is that note?" He'll play that note. And then the next, and then the next. We can take one step at a time, garnering wisdom from each emotion, as we become clear.

Match.com

Against all expert advice, I jumped right into online dating after we decided to divorce. I had been desiring a close, loving partnership for so long, and once my co-parent and I decided that would not be our partnership, I wanted to get the ball rolling. So I took some pictures, wrote up a profile, and started looking around. I signed up for Match and Bumble accounts but started with Bumble so I could hide until I wanted to be seen by someone I liked. In the few months after my co-parent moved out of the house, I went on several dates, wore myself out, and decided to set it down. During that same time, I was doing the psychedelic journeys and integration and starting to wonder if I did, actually, want a partner. As I was finding more and more love within, maybe all I wanted was me.

One night after watching a movie about a mother reuniting with her estranged son, I felt deep sadness that I would never have that chance with my mom. Taking the mushrooms' directive, I tapped into this sadness and had a heart-wrenching grieving session at my dining table, picturing my loved ones there with me, desperately looking to each one for connection and finding no one's glance meeting mine. It has been an intensely lonely life of offering myself and my love to others who didn't seem to want it.

I went for a walk to sorrowful music to continue the processing. And while on that walk, I heard a voice: "You are alone."

Well, yeah, duh, I know this.

"You need to plant more seeds."

Fine, whatever that means.

I got home from my walk, sat on my kitchen floor, and checked my email, finding one from Match.com. The voice continued. "Check Match."

Are you kidding?

No response. So I did, and when the first profile popped up, the voice said, "Check him out." I had seen this handsome winemaker's profile previously and did not feel led to reach out. Strike 1: winemaker. I am not a big drinker and figured he was. (Just drugs for me!) Strike 2: exclamation points. He wrote all sorts of things on his profile that would have been interesting if true. "At the end of a long day, I love sitting down for a thoughtful conversation over a glass of wine!!!" But I took his generous use of exclamation points as, "I'm full of shit!!!"

So my brain had said, without hesitation, *No thanks.*

But this voice, whoever's it was, told me that I had made the wrong choice. This man had unintentionally included a picture with a name tag showing his full name on it, so I was able to find an interview of him at his winery with his two boys. Hearing him speak, watching his movements, I felt drawn to him.

"Contact him."

No! At this point my profile was hidden on Match, and I was not ready to open those floodgates.

Again: "Contact him."

Ugh, fine. So I did what any reasonable person would do: I cold-call emailed this dude at his place of work to express romantic interest.

"Hi _____,

I happened upon your match.com profile tonight—I am not yet up for the onslaught that comes with going visible but thought your profile was interesting enough to try to be in touch otherwise.

I graduated from Penn, have my own consulting practice in the finance world, and have a very sweet almost-six-year-old son. I teach (free) barre classes for neighborhood moms in my driveway in Irvington. My passion is trauma healing, and I've had some extraordinary experiences with guided psychedelic journeys this year. Very kind and supportive co-parenting situation. Screen shot of my match profile below . . . if I don't hear from you, no sweat! All the best to you and your family!"

Well, friends, turns out he was a neighbor. Which means he did respond! And—his Match.com account was old, so he would never have received my message if I had not awkwardly—nay, boldly—emailed him at his winery's tasting request email. Subject Line: "Not a wine tasting request!"

———

Over the next week, I exchanged several emails with the guy I would ultimately nickname "the wine guy" before we decided to get together for a drink. We found each other on the sidewalk outside a Northeast Portland cocktail bar, and he held the door open for me, asking me how my week was going. As I answered, he turned toward me with a palpable energy. He was intensely present and curious. I could feel my energy settle in my core because I wasn't worried he was elsewhere, I wasn't chasing his attention—he was right here with me. We traded questions and stories at an engagingly quick clip. When I told him my latest theory on why my marriage didn't work, his unapologetic, straight-to-the-point insights took my breath away.

So I was disappointed when date two lacked the magic of our first meeting, feeling more like an unemotional exchange of information. As we walked away from the bar toward our cars, I accepted that this would not go further. We walked by his car first and stopped for a goodbye hug. Then it happened. A burst of energy moved through my body during that hug, screaming that this was right. I didn't know how to hold these two opposing experiences—a conversation that was not energizing alongside a hug that was electric—but I was intrigued.

And our meetings continued in this way, not always synching up in conversation. I remember sitting across from him at my dining table debating something I cared little about with a huge, unexplainable smile on my face. He asked what I was smiling about, and I said, "I don't know! I'm just happy." There was an energetic pull that kept me engaged. Before, I had internalized the message not to get swept away by the physical connection in romantic relationships. But I was also starting to learn how the body contains its own wisdom and that the stories crafted by our protective egos can be so far from what is true.

We had a bumpy few months. Early on, we had a conversation where he reflected back to me, without judgment, that I talk a lot about my trauma. There were times prior to this conversation where I worried there may be misalignment, like when he encouraged me to move toward the positive rather than spending all my time on the hard stuff. I was not looking for his advice—and—I thought he might be bypassing. So I kindly told him I wasn't sure this was a fit. I told him my courage and strength around healing my trauma were my best selling points, and if he wasn't interested in that, then there may not be much common ground. He said there was so much more to me than my trauma. But he wasn't interested in convincing me of this and wished me well.

In that moment, hearing something in his voice, I realized I had made a mistake. His energy was so clean— respectful and self-responsible. And he reflected back to me something I could not yet understand but that resonated:

There's more to me than my pain. Later that day, I reached out and asked for another chance.

Friends and loved ones did not hide their skepticism. "He can't handle the trauma." "You need someone whose childhood wounding is closer to yours so you can be more compatible." But I wasn't sure about that. It felt like he was offering me the chance to join him in a world I had not known but longed to. I had spent years giving myself love and compassion for my childhood trauma, an unquestionably critical part of my healing. And now I was ready for the next phase of my journey. I didn't want a partner who would accommodate my pain anymore, I wanted a partner who would help me stretch toward who I was meant to be.

When his communication was sparse and we had long stretches between hangouts, friends would say, "Surely he is seeing other women. He's not interested." But I tried to keep open because I knew this was a story, which may or may not be true. I wanted to rewire so that I acted from my intuition and not my fear.

My best friend was the only one in my life—including my therapist!—who did not display outward concern about my pursuing this relationship. She is otherworldly wise and very gifted at seeing the larger picture, and I think she also knew I might end up with this man and didn't want to position herself against that outcome. I knew the others in my life were just lovingly protective of me. I had been through so much, and they didn't want me to get hurt. But my paradigm had changed. It was no longer my goal to avoid pain, I wanted to pursue love. Part of this shift was from the voice in the woods—what I had been doing wasn't working. And part was that I had faced so much pain that I knew I could handle whatever was to come.

Let me be clear. This was a manual, slow, awkward rewiring. People talk about how spiritual awakenings are envisioned as blissful, meditative, light-shining-down events but in reality they can feel more like psychosis. Instead of the graceful caterpillar-to-butterfly transformation, I felt like I had ingested Polyjuice Potion from the Harry Potter series— insides writhing, skin bubbling, feet in agony in shoes now too small. At every decision, my default was to go left, but I made myself turn right. The turning right was based on my intuition. I just wasn't used to following my intuition, to pursuing what I desire.

And did I desire this man! I watched with utter confusion how much I wished we would run into each other in the neighborhood (which we somehow never did), how much my heart lifted when I'd see his name flash across my phone. My brain was like, *Lex, what the hell. You barely know this guy.* So when I'd get an indication that my interest was not reciprocated, I'd let go of my attachment. I'd feel a depth of sadness that I couldn't understand but could honor, and I'd let it go.

But, as this was all happening in the midst of my psychedelic journeys, repeatedly during those journeys I would hear the message that there was good here, not to let it go. So I'd get back on the horse and ask to meet up again.

Borrowing Dimensionality

When I was in elementary school, I was thrilled to play parts in the local community theater's productions of *Annie*, *The Best Christmas Pageant Ever*, and *James and the Giant Peach*. I have only one memory of my mom through all of my theater experience, and it was that she picked me up one night from play practice and had brought some Arby's curly fries for me. I'm not saying that was her only involvement, it's just all I remember. I don't remember her running lines with me, helping me get ready, celebrating my performances. And I don't have any pictures of me in any of these productions that would evidence an adoring audience. What I do remember viscerally was the shame I felt when my costume wasn't clean. We rehearsed in a Methodist church across the street from the theater, and one night I recall being alone in a side room getting dressed for rehearsal, sitting on a pew and pulling on dirty pantyhose. I was so grossed out by myself—can others tell? What would they think if they knew the truth about me?

Thirty years later, I took my son to Maui for my first big vacation as a single parent. I was his only entertainment for the week, so I didn't manage to find any time to relax or take care of myself during the trip. I made sure he had the outfits he needed while my practice with myself was to wear whatever I had, even if it didn't fit well or was worn out. When we were walking into an ice cream shop to buy him a treat, my only pair of flip-flops broke. I paid for his ice cream and walked outside, barefoot and deflated, crossing the hot asphalt toward our rental car.

I was asked after the trip whether we went to any fun restaurants, whether I had any yummy tropical beverages to mark the vacation. Nope, my son was in the mood for toast and nothing else that week, so we went out only once, to an order-at-the-counter type restaurant in a strip mall. He didn't want anything off the menu—not even French fries or dessert!—so when my sandwich arrived, he asked me how long it would take me to eat it. Wearily, I responded, "I don't know, maybe five minutes?" So he started counting down the seconds, "1, 2, 3…" I snapped, "DO. NOT. COUNT." The photos of this trip show a cute-as-can-be six-year-old and an exhausted and tattered me.

I have always been told I seem so put together. I unconsciously mastered this image. After a lifetime of neglect, I knew how to get by with the bare minimum to show people

I was on top of it, to prove that I belonged. But sometimes, as on this vacation, the top layer has not been robust enough to hide the neglect underneath. So entering a new relationship was a scary prospect—we could only get so close before I would be exposed as an imposter.

My take was that the wine guy was impressive and that I had to up my game to be at his level. Why did I think this? Oh, maybe it was the time that he ran a marathon and, when his Achilles tendon ruptured at mile twenty-two, he hopped the last four miles. I noticed a desire to qualify for his affection, and I judged this. I am lovable as I am and do not need to change for anyone. And I did the stuff anyway. I started running more. I ate better. I invested in my wardrobe, and I bought some goddamn nightstands after going without for months. One night when I planned to take a bath, he asked me if I was going to light a candle and put on some music. "Of course," I said, and then I scrambled to find a candle and a speaker.

But I was also just so inspired by him. One day I told him I wanted to go for a run but it was getting too hot. And he responded, "I hate it when people say it's too hot to run. Find some shade, pour some water on yourself, walk if you need, but don't miss the run!" And what I heard from him was not an ounce of judgment but encouragement to find possibility. At the root of my not wanting to run when it's too hot is fear. That I won't be okay, that I won't make it somehow. So I went for a run that day. And over and over I have practiced this, noting my fear but proceeding anyway, and over time my fears have gotten quieter and my desires have gotten louder.

While I initially thought I was changing to qualify for the wine guy's affection, what sustained these changes was that I saw myself in his reflection. I was drawn to his zest for life, to his creativity, to his pursuit of joy. These things were ready to come out in me. I love being out in nature, being physically active, and taking better care of my body. Turns out I find nightstands quite useful. Baths with candles and music *are* so nice. And I am thrilled to see possibility where I used to see limitations—like strapping on some ice cleats and going for a run during an ice storm, whereas before I would have felt stuck indoors and frustrated.

The efforts I made to keep up with him helped me stop neglecting myself. I started filling out as a person instead of showing up—for me and for others—as just the surface layer. I learned that I am so much stronger than I thought I was when I was stuck in my fear.

It doesn't matter if these efforts started out with a different outcome in mind, one that I didn't need by the end. This motivation was just a road to travel on for a bit to help me discover these previously unacknowledged parts of myself and how much more I could do to love and care for myself.

I Want More

Years ago, a friend of mine was running the Hood-to-Coast overnight relay race, a two-hundred-mile race that starts at the top of Mount Hood and ends at the ocean in Seaside, Oregon. The typical team will have twelve runners, who will each run three five- or six-mile legs. A talented athlete himself, my friend tells the story about a man who ran up from behind him during his overnight leg and began chatting with him. They ran together for a minute or so, and then this kind stranger said, "Okay, let's do this!" and ran off into the darkness at an incredible pace.

I'd later joke that this stranger was the wine guy because he runs competitively in that race and because this was the role he played for me. When friends would ask me how things were going with him, I'd say he was basically my life coach. He showed up in my life to inspire and encourage me and—any moment now—would run off into the night. I figured the universe led me to him to have some fun and heal some stuff in preparation for my next, for-real relationship. I thought this because, while the wine guy saw lots of good in me—sometimes more than I could see—he also seemed to be oblivious to some parts of me. What I didn't realize then was that this was my doing, not his. I didn't know how much I was still hiding.

One night, about six months into hanging out, we had an authentic moment during dinner that shifted things. He was telling me about his holiday plans with his kids—a two-week skiing road trip following snow storms around the Pacific Northwest—and I reflected back to him what a special adventure he was creating for his kids. His eyes lit up, like, *You get it*. We connected in that moment, and the rest of the evening was softer, more trusting, more vulnerable. When I got into my car after our date, I thought, *Shit, I really like him*.

I had a psilocybin journey the following week, and this was the first time I did not get a message to keep things going. My feeling coming away from that journey was that I needed to honor myself. I couldn't keep this casual, sporadic thing going if I really liked him. I told him that I was looking for more, and I was ready for that to be the end. But he responded that, while he didn't realize it before then, he didn't want to let this go. He wanted more too.

And the wine guy became my partner.

Over and over, though, I would come against an edge. As my feelings for him grew, I would realize that I was not showing up fully. This would present in the form of anger—like I was pissed at him for not seeing me. But that anger was not about him, it was my being screaming, *I don't want to hide anymore!*

I have gone through all my life with the unconscious baseline assumption that others are too fragile for me to show up fully. To avoid facing my lack of control around my mother's demise, it had to be about me. And she had to have been so fragile that whatever I did—as a delightful, innocent child—led to her depression, her addiction, and her death. This muted me, paralyzed me. I could never offer my perspective, my truth to another without the fear that it could send them over the edge. I could not show up as the full version of myself because the worst-case scenario would ensue.

But I didn't realize any of this. I didn't know how much I was hiding to keep others safe (which in turn kept me safe so they didn't die and leave me).

So I internalized my quiet as meaning that I didn't have anything to say. And I internalized my lack of excellence as meaning that I didn't have anything worthy to contribute.

After the psychedelic journeys and all of the internal work, I was starting to get in touch with the goodness I had unconsciously locked away, and increasingly I couldn't tolerate playing small like I always had. Every time I approached my partner with a warning—"Get ready, I'm going to up my game, you ain't seen nothin' yet"—I would brace for his departure. Instead, to my amazement, his emphatic, unwavering response was, "BRING IT." I'd reveal more, and he'd love what I'd reveal.

Being more fully me with my partner has been outrageously fun and so goddamn relieving. Early on, I'd experience instances where he would exhaustively explain something, and I'd sit there with an internal eye roll and note how he did not value or see me. I thought my pain around this was tied to his opinion of me—he didn't think I was smart enough. But, no! The pain was that I was playing small because I thought *he* was too fragile to handle my response. It wasn't being talked down to, it was the hiding that was painful. My partner and I are equal-opportunity offenders here, as we both have a tendency to overexplain things to each other. Now, grounded in my wisdom and strength— and knowing how open-minded and resilient he is—I'll put on my faux confused voice and say, "I'm so sorry, this is really hard to track, can you explain this once more . . . ?" And we'll both crack up at it. It is exhilarating to stand tall and revel in our reflection of each other's strength instead of playing small in reaction to a fragility that I projected onto him.

The Love Is My Love

In the early days of our relationship, I experienced a lot that felt neglectful or abandoning. Something as simple as not having a text acknowledged or going days between communications could trigger me. I had felt led to this relationship, and I knew deep down that there was more to harvest here, so leaving the relationship behind did not feel like the right call. But I was frustrated and skeptical—what is the value in this? I thought the whole point of entering into a new relationship was to not repeat the patterns of my childhood so I could heal those wounds. I've often heard "You can't heal in isolation," and I was looking for someone else to treat me in a different way so I could heal.

But I'd pull back my energy in those exchanges and set better boundaries to find a better balance. The waters would settle, and I'd feel comforted that I was moving beyond the neglect and abandonment. The learning I took away was that I could protect myself by making good choices in relationship. If I chose the right partner or set the right boundaries, I could protect myself. I saw the gift of these small abandonments as learning how to protect myself from a larger abandonment. Get hurt a little to protect myself from bigger hurt.

Nine months into our relationship, after we had exchanged *I love you*'s and I was much more invested, my partner asked for some time apart. The request was made respectfully, referencing feeling drained energetically without blame or judgment, with an openness to coming back together after some time. Still, it felt like a sudden and devastating abandonment—one that I clearly had not been able to foresee and protect myself against. I knew enough to play it kind of cool, not to push it or go on the attack, even though I felt blindsided.

Instead, I watched my emotions, which were painful and plentiful, including feeling rejected, fearful that love could disappear in an instant, sad at the potential loss of my partner, not trusting that there were others out there. I was introduced to Dr. Sue Morter's central channel breathing, which she describes in her book *The Energy Codes*. Dr. Morter is an expert in bio-energetic medicine, and her breathwork helps integrate some of these old, stuck energies and emotions. On top of feeling heartache, I had intense pain in my left shoulder. Because the pain felt almost unbearable,

I did this breathwork for hours, day and night. The physical pain would subside, and I would find peace and clarity. Until the next wave, at which point I would start again.

In my earlier line of thinking—that I can have stronger boundaries, make better choices, protect myself—I would have demanded, *Why do I need to experience this again, and in such a painful way?* But I have learned to see every experience as a gift. This set of circumstances was not a static blow to which I was victim but an opportunity to look inward.

With the help of this breathwork, I discovered I was looking to my partner to meet needs that are my responsibility. The idea that we cannot heal in isolation does not mean that I cannot heal myself, that I need others to meet my needs or to show me how. It means I need the triggers, both joyful and painful. The love I felt when I was with my partner was love that was already within me. The sadness I felt when my partner wanted space was sadness that was already within me. Being in relationship with another helps me access what needs to be integrated and augmented— my ability to generate and receive love—and what needs to be integrated and healed—in this case, my sadness. Once revealed, my solo work begins.

My responses to his request for space included a slew of "I" statements. I appreciate the feedback; I respect where you are and wish you all you desire; I am grateful for our time together; and, ultimately, I am unattached. By the time I had worked through all of this, I was truly unattached. I realized I had within everything I needed, so I would welcome more time with my partner and would be fine if we had seen each other for the last time.

Before, my energy was dispersed: I thought about my partner with great frequency, looked to him for feedback, deferred to him. I was still in the practice of sitting at the kitchen table—of being unilaterally available in hopes of affection. When I pulled my energy back to me with the help of *The Energy Codes*, anchoring in my body, there were two immediate transformations. First, I discovered vital parts of me that were previously unknowable given my outward focus. One creative breakthrough was this book— while I had never once contemplated being a writer, I woke up one day and words started flooding out of me. Second, my partner no longer needed space. He could feel the energetic shift. Dr. Morter explains that "when we throw all our energy and attention onto something or someone, it actually pushes them away. . . . Shifting our focus from outside ourselves to inside ourselves—from object to subject—makes all the difference in the results we get in relationships, and in creative endeavors."

On my path, I transitioned first from tolerating the neglect and abandonment that I'd always experienced; next to taking more of an active role in creating boundaries and making sure I was taken care of; and finally to understanding that the pieces that were out of my control—that would hurt the most, that I couldn't protect myself against—would bring me the biggest gift. I broke through. I realized that I am the source of my love, that I am all that I need, and that I don't need anyone else to heal. It was within me the whole time. I could take the feeling of love that I had felt with my partner and generate that feeling in my body. I could breathe it through my whole body and into the world.

Are You My Mother?

My second psilocybin journey felt like a slow-motion trudging through my childhood trauma. After, I wondered if I had to intentionally retrace every instance of trauma to be able to heal. But, no, I can rely on my triggers to bring up the stuff that needs to be looked at, that I'm ready to look at. As in P. D. Eastman's children's book *Are You My Mother?*, I find opportunity after opportunity where my subconscious is trying to work out my childhood pain with whichever people and circumstances are in front of me. Consciously, I think I am experiencing something entirely new, but it is really about my mother.

After finding a mass in my breast, I had a prolonged period of diagnosis before finding out it was benign—and ample opportunity to move through the roller coaster of emotions. First, I was gutted by the possibility that I could die and leave my son. There is an oft-stated sentiment that we should not worry until we have something to worry about. But I knew the emotions that were surfacing were here to teach me something.

I had vats of sadness within about potentially leaving my child behind. If I were grounded in love and the knowing that everything is okay, I would not hold it in this way. I had such sorrow from being left by my mom, such fear that my son would not be okay without me. And this mass was the loving trigger to let me know this. To help more come to the surface and be released so that I could find a deeper sense of safety and love. I was projecting my feelings of weakness and vulnerability from my trauma onto my son instead of seeing him as the extraordinarily strong being that he is. I was projecting my fear that things would not be okay onto a universe in which things are okay. Just as they are.

The next emotional wave was fear that having cancer could mean the end of my relationship with my partner. We were only a year in, and he had just lost his mom to cancer. It was a lot. But he said he's here for it all.

Via text—the most effective way to gauge tone, right?—I asked to spend time with him the evening the pathology report was due.

Me: "Free next Thursday evening? Should have results by then—biopsy Tuesday morning."

My partner: "Thursday works perfectly as Wednesday I have a fundraising meeting!"

My interpretation: So if he had a conflict on Thursday, he would not make space for me if I found out I have cancer?

My emotional response: What the actual fuck.

Thankfully my higher self got a word in as my younger part was freaking out, so I was aware that sometimes I am lost in my story and that there *might* be different energy on his side. I checked in with my partner. Nope, I didn't pick up the phone, kept going with text.

"I trust you didn't mean it to land this way . . . sounds like you're saying my potential cancer diagnosis would be convenient for you on Thursday but not Wednesday. . . ."

His response was not immediate, and during that quiet space before I heard from him, I was spewing with anger. At all the stories I believed were true, including nuclear options about our relationship.

As I felt immense anger toward him, I was able to tap into the knowing that this anger was not actually about him at all. The way I interpreted his response was just the trigger to help emotions that were ready to come up, stuck energy that was ready to move. Right now. This is the gift. This stuff was buried a day ago, and now it's saying, *Let's do this.*

So I stayed with me, did my central channel breathing, and remained curious about what this was all about. Part of the anger was a younger version of me who was so pissed she had to carry so much alone. *Why can't you help me? Why am I not the priority?* The story she took away was that she was not lovable enough to prioritize and that her needs were unimportant. So I offered her the true story, that she is so beautifully worthy of love and support. Any messaging otherwise stemmed from others' struggles and wasn't about her. *I am here with you. I've got you. You do not have to hold this alone. In fact, I am deeply honored to be a part of this journey with you. To watch your grace as you accept this potential reality, your desire to heal so that you discover more love, your commitment to finding beauty and light and humor in all of it.* And the piece I sometimes forget is pausing enough for her to take this in. She is seen, held, celebrated, cherished. Breathe that through.

And the anger started to resolve. And I got back to the energy I felt before this trigger, which was less attached to the role my partner or others would play, grounded in my immense capacity and the knowing that I am safe and surrounded by love. I felt grateful for whatever path was ahead of me, humbled by the continuing, unfolding beauty.

And what felt simultaneously like *Of course* and *Are you kidding me?* was that when I did talk with my partner, he was clear that he'd rearrange anything in his schedule any time to be there with and for me. Misunderstanding his text was a textbook example of seeing through the lens of my childhood. I used to have a sweet but judgmental reaction to this—a compassionate *There I go again* given my wounding. But it's not to be judged! These were the ingredients for transformation. This was a critical misinterpretation, leading me to be in touch with this part of me who needed to be seen and loved. And she will be forever changed because she was. That is, the energy will be forever changed, and I will relate to the world differently.

And while I am a staunch advocate for finding healing within, my partner was more loving, more effusive, more committed than I anticipated in our conversation. I know his love does not sustain me, as it does have to come from within me, but I am taking notes on how to better love myself when his love exceeds what I thought was possible.

Getting Out of My Way

My partner and I were sitting on the steps outside the lodge at Breitenbush Hot Springs, a healing retreat center in the Cascade mountain range in Oregon. It was a sunny March day, and while there was still snow on the ground, the warmth of the natural hot springs melted the snow in the yard just in front of the lodge. A few deer had stumbled upon this exposed grass and settled in for some nourishment. A black cat named Magic approached the deer, and they investigated each other carefully. People would walk by—respectfully and quietly, of course—but the deer were unfazed by their human counterparts, peacefully making their way around this patch of paradise.

I have always filled my time less than others, and I'm ready to hang longer when the other person says, "I gotta go!" I saw that as a knock on me—geez, I need to have more going on. After a weekend of relaxing and recharging at Breitenbush, we were due back home. And when my partner turned to say something to me, I was sure he was going to say, "I need to get going." Instead, my heart melted when he asked, "Can we sit here a bit longer?"

Where else is there to be when bald eagles are flying overhead? When the deer are so close you can hear them chew?

I feel so much genuine, deep joy when I'm with my partner. I laugh all the time. The things I was drawn to on our first date—his presence and curiosity—are a continual invitation for me to be awake and alive. He is a relentless mirror for me, not letting a single word pass without thoughtful receipt. I am constantly, delightfully caught off guard with his quick intellect. Despite his generous use of exclamation points, which it turns out are an accurate reflection of his zest for life, he can seem very serious much of the time. So when I get a chuckle out of him, it is one of my favorite sounds in the world.

I have been skeptical of how good it feels when he calls me sweet names like "pumpkin" or "darling," not wanting to rely on him to compensate for some deficiency in my childhood. And maybe I would have wanted more of this kind of sweetness in my childhood. But I also talk to myself like that—that's my energy for me. So I'm not fed by it in the way that I need someone else to provide it to me, but I am sure fed by being with someone who can love me the way I love me. And his hugs! His hugs.

So, as time went on, I had no desire for our relationship to end. My partner was clear that he wanted to live together. I didn't have clarity otherwise, so that's where we headed. But when we were getting closer to moving in together, I became really scared that I couldn't handle it. I do not have a history of living easefully with loved ones. With my childhood neglect, I am wired to scan my surroundings always, desperately needing attunement and looking for danger. I was not aware of this previously, as my co-parent gave me ample space to not get triggered in this way.

But now, having a present, active partner with two active kids overwhelmed my hypervigilant nervous system. A year and a half into our relationship, we went on our first week-long vacation with the kids, and I was a mess. I was so distracted by my partner and his kids that I was not clued into what my son and I needed. So I didn't take good care of our duo, and I took my difficulties out on my partner. From his perspective, it sucked to have me make him responsible for me. From my perspective, I just didn't know how we could live together without me losing myself and my ability to care for my son and me. I wondered if this was the right partnership for me, or if living with any partner would ever be right for me.

And in my hesitation, we started to crack.

———

I worried my partner and I may not be right for each other. But I also knew that if we were and I made a misstep here, I could lose something that I had desired for so long—and someone unlike anyone I had ever known. So I signed up for an Ayahuasca ceremony the week after our vacation and did tons and tons of meditation and breathwork to try to get clear. I asked Mother Aya to give me more perspective around our relationship. During the ceremony, I saw reflections of all of the things I already knew: I love my partner dearly and adore his kids, I would be so sad if this ended, and some pieces around merging our families are really scary and painful for me. Great, thanks. Super helpful.

I started to see the repeat of my lifelong wounds of losing those I loved. This made me question my spiritual journey—who the fuck cares if I was led by divine guidance to a man I loved if I lose him so quickly? Is any of this worth it if things are always changing and you lose the beauty you discover?

But in the days and weeks that followed Ayahuasca, I became aware that what was painful about our relationship had nothing to do with my partner. I realized I was still not showing up fully, authentically, because I was scared to lose him. When he said he wanted to move in together, I didn't pause to get clear about what I wanted. I just went along with it, fearful that if I didn't, he would no longer want to be with me. I hoped that, because I loved him, living together was the right call. What I didn't realize was that as long as I acted from my fear of losing him, as long as I had any willingness to contort myself to be loved by my partner, I would never be able to joyfully merge our families and our lives.

There was a time during the Ayahuasca ceremony where my body melted away, and I basked in my essence. It was indescribably blissful, one of the most beautiful experiences of my life. Coming away from that experience, my love for and dedication to myself overshadowed the need to be loved by my partner. And as the fear of losing him quieted, what remained was the goodness we shared—the presence, the sweetness, the joy, the laughter. I felt deeply grounded in my capacity to handle any growth areas that would come with living together. I knew then that I wanted to move forward together.

———

We were sitting at our neighborhood coffee shop during a winter storm. The door was jammed, allowing frigid air to seep in, so we kept on our hats and puffer jackets to stay warm. After some small talk over tea, we quieted for the main event. I reached out for my partner's hand, looked into his eyes and said, "I want to move forward with you." He looked at me for a moment and then averted his eyes toward the wintry weather outside, biting his lip. I could tell he didn't want to hurt me.

We had been in contact since our family vacation but less frequently. The *I love you*'s had dropped off. As I was desperately trying to get clear, I felt my partner pulling away. And when we got together at the coffee shop, my suspicions were confirmed. After a moment, he turned back from the window and said, "I just don't know, Alexis. I'm not con-vinced you do know what you want."

I countered, "I *do*. I have done the work to get clear. But I can understand why you may not feel convinced of this yet." We ended our conversation with expressions of our love for each other. We said we'd be in touch and hugged each other goodbye.

I felt grounded during our coffee shop conversation. But as time went on, my abandonment wounding surfaced with a vengeance. This time, since we were further along in our relationship—kids in the mix, planning on moving in together—I felt more inclined to do something about it than before. I wanted to say, "You can't leave the relationship!" I wanted to convince him of why he wouldn't want to leave. I wanted to judge him for leaving. I wanted to shut down the relationship myself.

And it felt terrible. It felt terrible to lose him either from my shutting it down or expecting him to shut it down. From seeing the singular path forward as the tragic loss of love. It felt so much better to me when I just held out possibility for what might happen. I honored the love that was there. And how big and beautiful and real it was. I honored it as something that was not to be contained in a rigid closure of this chapter. I didn't have a specific path forward, and I knew I didn't have to. I knew if I remained open and loving, then something beautiful would unfold.

This was a constant effort to rewire. I would wake up in the morning, sad or hurt about the potential loss of this relationship. I would get out my computer and write furiously about everything that was wrong and doomed. And then I would notice that defeated energy and remember that I had found my way to something truer. I would make my way again to this new clearing, grounded in my knowing, holding space for possibility. All of the scary things from my history of abandonment resurfaced—that love disappears, that I am not lovable—and I deepened into my knowing that our love was and is true, tender, breathtaking. I could stare, right in the face, my partner's inclination that there may not be a path forward. I could hear his concerns about our compatibility and be unattached to how he worked through that. I didn't have the same question. I had the question of whether I could show up in love.

During this time, I borrowed from my future self. I knew that in some time, I would not feel the pain of this, that I would have found healing. So when we'd have an interaction, I'd notice my default reaction that was grounded in fear, and I would ask myself how my future, healed self would react instead. And that's where I'd come from—a peaceful, loving, grateful place. Once after days of silence, he reached out with a text saying, "I hope you had a nice weekend!" And I wanted to ignore it or be short in response. Because I was hurt by the days of silence, by the distance when I desired closeness. Instead, I imagined the future, healed me, who would be grateful for the kind sentiment, and from that feeling of genuine gratitude, I thanked him for the kindness.

When I shared the current happenings with others— some loved ones, some advisors—I got the familiar protective response. Some held their opinions, but their shocked facial expressions said it all: *What is he thinking, risking losing you?* Another was more direct, suggesting that he had already left me, so I should move on. Tears streamed down my cheeks as she said, "Alexis, surely you don't want to move forward with him." That conversation flattened me. I thought that was because, according to her, I had to lose this person I loved. But it wasn't. I was flattened because I supplanted my knowing with her fearful projection.

I am meant to live from a place of love. Everything that was rigid and bracing was cutting me off from my own essence. So I didn't need to be attached to coming back together with my partner, but I did need to be firmly planted in a place of creativity, of trust, of knowing that love can transform things in beautiful, unfathomable ways. As long as I supplanted what felt true to me with someone else's fearful, protective approach, nothing in my life could feel full and robust. I would dance or write or sing, but what good is any of it when I am so disconnected from myself? I would feel boundlessly unsafe. When I reject my truth, there is no place for me to be. But as soon as I returned to love, I felt held and safe and blissful.

And by the time I worked through all of this, the potential for loss had a different quality—it didn't feel as much like loss because I did not lose the love or the possibility.

———

My partner and I started spending time together again, and it was clear to me that his love for me had not waned in our time apart. He would pull me onto his lap and hold me tight. We would fall asleep with our fingers lovingly interlocked.

One morning, I shared with a friend that I thought we were coming back together. And hours later, I was sitting at my dining table when my partner called to tell me he put an offer on a house in a neighboring city and planned to move there with his boys. It was such a casual relay of information, as if I wouldn't be shattered by the news that the man I loved and wanted to live with had chosen to move on with his life without me. Of course, I was shattered, and I immediately launched into my central channel breathing to try to integrate my energy and ground myself in our conversation.

"I'm just trying to catch up here," I managed.

"Catch up on what?"

"We planned on buying a house together. And now you are moving without me."

"I have wanted to move for a long time. And I held off on that for you. But when our future became less settled, my move became priority again. This is a unique opportunity, a great house for my boys and me."

"I honor that. And I also have a vision of us together. I see us being married. So it is difficult to see you going in a different direction."

It was time to pick up our kids from school, so the conversation ended soon thereafter, with some levity and kindness. But I was thrown. The next day I flew to Maui for a solo trip, and I was exhausted and ready to give up. I had put it all out there. I had remained open and loving, and it just wasn't coming together.

My partner called as I was walking into a grocery store on Maui to get food for my trip. I rolled my eyes as he shared that the offer he placed on the house had been accepted—*Do you need me to be an audience for this?* But then he pivoted, saying he appreciated what I had said the day before.

"Which part?"

"That you see us together, that you see us married."

"Did you not know that?"

"You've never said that before."

He was right. I had not shared that because I was scared—too scared to even admit it to myself. What if I was wrong? What if I hurt him or his kids or my kid? Even saying it now scared me. But it was the truth that emerged from loving possibility. And my honoring that truth had been a missing piece to the puzzle.

———

The day after I finally put all my cards on the table, my partner opened back up to me. He said he wanted to move forward together.

But he didn't immediately cancel the contract to buy the new house, one that was too small for all of us. I did my best to continue my newfound practice of being unattached, grounded in love, remaining curious rather than believing the worst-case stories in my head—that he still had a foot out the door.

One day I asked him how to reconcile these two seemingly competing energies—wanting to be with me for the rest of his days, alongside this still-open path toward a house that didn't work for our combined family. Frustrated, he said, "This is a time for me to celebrate what I've accomplished. It has been a very long, very hard road, and I am finally in a place to make this happen for my boys. Conversations like this distract from that celebration."

I responded, "I *want* to celebrate you. I think it is amazing what you have created. I'm just trying to understand how our paths can come back together here."

Impatiently, he shot back, "Maybe we just shelve all of this."

Gut punch. He did have a foot out the door.

Here I was again. Feeling the heartbreak I knew so well, not being enough for those I loved to stick around, to fight for me. But then I caught myself. I can stick around, I can fight for me. I *am* enough. I tapped into all the goodness that I've uncovered along this journey. And from that place of power and love, I responded, "You know, in a number of years, when you are out in the dating world and you still haven't met someone like me, you might look back on this conversation and wish you had been a little more patient."

The line went silent. And then he came back on and said, "You're right. I'm sorry."

That night at dinner, he pulled me in close and said, "I heard you today. I'm all in. I'm sorry it took me so long to trust you again."

The next day, he cancelled the contract on the new house, and a couple of months later, he and his boys moved into our home.

———

Lots had to line up for me to meet my partner—he had to include his last name accidentally in his dating profile pictures; I had to reach out to him at his winery because I have no fear of being awkward, not knowing he no longer checked his Match.com account anyway; and I had to have a voice from the heavens tell me to ignore my initial warning signs and move forward. He has said to me how unlikely it is that we found each other—it can feel like you just got by, barely—but I believe it was all orchestrated. I called him in.

The trick, though, is that I have to keep calling him in. Every day I have the choice of the energy I put out into the world. The energy I invest in this relationship. I can come from a place of guardedness, of fear, and that pushes my partner away. Or I can bring my immense love and creativity, and that draws him to me.

When this all started, the part of me that was ready to love imagined a beautiful partnership with a powerfully loving man. That part of me signaled to my partner that I was ready to create with him. And when I become immersed in my fear, I am telling him I can no longer meet him there.

But as I rewired and rewired and showed up day after day with openness and love, I called him back in.

One-for-a-Gazillion

I started looking inward in an effort to not have a tragic life. The way I saw that happening was that I would heal my wounds and no longer carry so much pain. And the absence of pain would, by definition, shift my equation—I would be happier without so much sadness. But the equation is so much more generous than that! It is not a one-for-one exchange, less sadness for more happiness. It is a one-for-a-gazillion exchange. When I am willing to feel my pain fully, the pain does ultimately go away. But the joy that comes with rediscovering myself is almost too much to bear.

I spent a lifetime thinking I was embarrassingly bad with words. I jumbled common idioms: "sharpest tool in the . . . wait, something about a lightbulb, er . . . maybe a doorknob?" I rushed my speech, certain I didn't have anything worthy to share. I delayed the required writing courses in college as long as I could, turning in what I was sure were terribly written and uninteresting pieces.

So I was astonished when I woke up one early morning to fully formed chapters leaping from my fingertips. I watched in awe as stories and insights of hopefulness and love flooded out of me. Stunned by this revelation, it took some time for it to soak in.

One day while walking in the woods, I tried it on, saying out loud to myself, "I am a writer." There was something so tender and sacred about this discovery—it felt like I was a mother who was reunited with her child after years of separation, learning what she grew up to be. Overcome with delight and gratitude, I wept, "You are a writer?" It was beyond my wildest dreams for myself to have grown up to be this person, to be living with such joy and creativity and connectedness.

I always thought my heartbreak was about losing my mom, but the most devastating part of my childhood was that I lost myself. When I numbed to survive the loss of my mother, I forgot that I was a writer. I lost my connection to my healing power and my loving essence. All these years when I was desperately looking for meaning and purpose, I was actually trying to find myself again, trying to remember who I am.

When my partner and I took space, I felt the grief of my childhood abandonment. For the first time in my life, I let the devastation wash over me. And because I was finally able to feel what I couldn't those many years ago, I woke up these parts of me that had been deeply asleep.

From spiritual teachers I've heard the question, "What are you doing to perpetuate your childhood wounds?" I internalized this as, *Dang it, I had this hard thing happen in my life, and I'm responsible for it continuing to happen.* Of course, I was grateful to understand that I could do it differently, to find newer, more loving patterns for myself. But the directive I took in was definitely to stop perpetuating those wounds.

Now, a different question has formed in my mind: "*Why* do you think you are perpetuating your childhood wounds?" I don't know that I was meant to stop perpetuating those wounds. In inviting the same painful circumstances into my life, I was giving myself a chance over and again to awaken these parts. To feel the pain and allow the beauty to return.

In my partnership, my being said, *I'm gonna hesitate here. I'm going to act in a way that will push my partner away, that will create the space and circumstances for these painful emotions to arise again. And I'm going to keep giving myself this chance until I rediscover the parts of me that were lost.*

Pain is not a distinct piece that goes away with healing. It is inextricably linked to unimaginable beauty that is hidden just underneath.

Who's the Teacher?

During the winter storm when my partner and I were taking space, we went sledding one day. As we were dragging the sled from my house to the sledding hill, he said that one of his arms was bothering him, and I jokingly asked if he was having a stroke. I playfully bumped up against him and asked, "Do you know who you are?"

He turned to me and said, deadpan but with a smidge of levity, "Oh, I know who *I* am."

I have felt hurt about how guarded my partner has been with me at times, about how he does not seem to trust who I say I am, what I say I want. But I have been in the washing machine of a spiritual awakening since I met him, not knowing which way is up much of the time.

I have gone through several rounds of transformations in our time together. Sure, when I get to the other side of an intensely transformative phase, I am a better partner—more grounded, more loving, more open. But I can't promise where I'll end up when I'm in the midst of the transformation, so how could it not unnerve him? When I frame it this way, I am honored that he has seen so much goodness in me to hang around while I have turned over every cell in my body.

On the other end of the spectrum, my partner has shown up as who he is, knowing what he wants, from the start. He says he has known who he is for a long time now. And I have worried that this translates to rigidity, that he is unopen to growth. How can we walk this meandering path together, grow together, if he already is who he is?

Well, first, I am always surprised about how open-minded and gracious he is in our conversations. But also, dear god, what else could work for me?

My partner has been a steady—if at times skeptical—rock, holding space as I dig more and more deeply into my wounds in pursuit of healing. Even when it was early in our relationship, after each psychedelic journey I craved a hug from him to help ground me back into my human life. And my soul is filled by the adventure and joy and beauty he shares with me. Taking in the gorgeous sunset from his hilltop vineyard, my arms wrapped tightly around his chest on the back of his ATV, driving through the vines and sampling the deliciously ripe grapes just ahead of harvest—this stuff fuels me so I can keep doing the hard work. During one of my journeys, the mushrooms showed me that the nutrients in our relationship were very much traveling from my partner to me.

In these pages I've been sharing a very detailed view into how I approach healing and growth. My partner doesn't approach it in the same way. This is not his road map. And yet, we often reach the same conclusion by our different paths, something we would miss if we were stuck on agreement every step of the way. And—we're all here to learn different lessons, so what is hard for me may not be hard for him, and vice versa. Sometimes I share a mind-blowing revelation with him, and his response is something akin to *Duh*. As I continue the work of releasing an attachment to a singular "way," I begin to be fed by the magical interplay of our differences.

Finding a Man

I have flown my nephew out to Portland since he was seven years old in an effort to support him and shower him with love. Because our family's legacy of trauma lives on, I wanted to share the insights and empowerment I was learning in case it could help him.

When he was seventeen, we were sitting at my dining room table, trading curse words as our gingerbread mansion's roof insisted on caving in. Between the cursing, I shared with him the latest in my spiritual journey, including how a voice picked my incredible partner off of Match.com.

He responded, "So you are saying all of this work is worth it so you can find a man?"

At first I was embarrassed by this—"Of course not! That's not what I mean!" But on second thought, yes, that's exactly what I mean. All of this is worth it so that I can have my dreams come true, and one of my dreams has been to be in a loving partnership. I have internalized that finding romantic love is silly or at least not feminist. I must be so weak to need a man in my life. But it's not about need. I can kick ass all by myself and have been doing that for years. But now I am looking to live a vibrant, unabashedly joyful life, and part of that for me is to have a kick-ass partner by my side to share the joy. And to trigger the hell out of me so I can keep growing and discovering more and more beauty within.

And also—our longings foreshadow what is to be, what is destined, so I offer a loving *fuck off* to any judgment of what I desire. I longed for all sorts of qualities in a partner, and my partner has those very qualities. Even weird things like an unexplained interest I developed in wine country in the year before I met him, and now I have a reason to be in wine country often. I used to think of this as getting what I wanted, but I believe my longing for this partnership was simply a knowing that I was headed in that direction.

Discovering and loving myself began well before I met my partner. But our relationship was the vehicle to deepen this work for me. During our time together, I have learned to listen to my intuition, disregarding others' opinions over and over to connect with my truth. I have come to life after hiding and playing small for forty years. I have learned what it means to love deeply and courageously in the face of the most terrifying pain of my life—being abandoned by the one I hold most dear—finding my way from a life directed by fear to a life grounded in my loving essence.

I have always adored the love song "Bloom" by the Paper Kites. The beautiful melody and utterly sweet and vulnerable lyrics capture the intimate, loving connection I have desired in partnership. And as I looked past my marriage toward my next potential partner, I imagined feeling this way in that relationship—feeling such closeness with my partner, filled with such sweetness by my partner, that he would be my world.

My partner and I love each other deeply, passionately. We have shared our amazement that what we've always wanted in partnership is possible, after thinking we needed to pick and choose which parts of ourselves to honor in selecting a partner. And—our love is icing on the cake. We come together in reflection and celebration of the love we each have for ourselves as a foundation. The kind of love portrayed in "Bloom," it turns out, is not the kind of love I was meant to have with another but with myself.

I fill myself with sweetness, my world is me.

Epilogue

So much in my life has felt magical in these last few years. Hearing the mysterious, benevolent guidance on occasion. Uncovering these incredible gifts that were completely unknown to me before. Experiencing more love than I ever imagined was possible.

And I have begun to see my power to share this magic with the world. It is always a little scary, always a risk that I will have put myself out there and no one will respond. But when I strum the loving string on my guitar, others' strings invariably vibrate in resonance. The goodness comes together.

I started tithing to that which feeds me spiritually, giving money to people who have helped me find a deeper connection to myself, to love. Talk about awkward—walking up and sharing how grateful I am for someone and handing them cash! But every single person has graciously accepted and has been blown away by the gratitude and the tithe, in many cases solving a stressful financial problem just in time for the recipient.

I notice that when I am feeling disconnected from my partner, contrary to my historical tendency to run for the hills, I need only lean into the relationship with love. And I watch how instantly the love acts like a fertilizer, bringing a burst of connectedness and gratitude and celebration.

I see how much my love can shape my relationship with my co-parent. Though, admittedly, I have not always been quite on the mark about my vision for our newly nontraditional family.

I desperately wanted to protect my son from the painful disconnection typical of divorce. One of my strategies to this end was that my co-parent and I would still spend holidays together and take family vacations together. So a few months after my co-parent moved out of the house, we went on vacation with our good friends to the San Juan islands in Washington state. One morning I was making chocolate chip pancakes, standing at the stove with spatula in hand, when my mind wandered to a vision of one day cooking with my co-parent's next partner. I wondered if it was possible to create an unusual but supportive, loving, connected dynamic for our nontraditional family. As a start, I thought our inaugural co-parenting vacation was going well! And when we got home, my co-parent said to me, "Well, I never need to do that again."

But other times the seeds I've planted have grown into something more exhilarating and beautiful than I could have imagined. When I first started my consulting company, I bought a luxury tote bag for my business meetings, with the purpose of communicating my value to new clients. I don't have these kinds of meetings anymore, so this purse has sat unused in my closet for years. I didn't want to sell it because I'd get so little money compared to its value, and I wondered if there might be someone in my life who would enjoy it.

I called my co-parent and said, "I know this is kinda weird, but would your partner like my tote bag?"

And instead of saying, "That *is* weird, and no, and why would you even think this is appropriate?" he said, "I'm not sure, I can ask her. I'd be happy to pay you for it."

I responded, "No, this is a gift. You and I bought that bag, and I would love for your partner to have it if she'd enjoy it."

He said, "Wow, that's so generous, thank you. Let me get back to you."

His partner graciously accepted, floored by the gesture and our kind and supportive co-parenting relationship.

At first glance this could seem like a one-off exchange involving an inconsequential item. But it was so much more than that—underneath the gesture was a spirit of generosity, an offering to set down the fear and guardedness common in divorce in order to forge a path of mutual trust and loving support. And in accepting the offering, my co-parent and his partner showed me, to my great delight, that we could create together in this space.

A week after the gift, we were all doing our best moves at my son's tae kwon do–themed birthday party, and the energy surrounding my son was not the disconnection I so feared initially but a coming together in easeful, joyful celebration. We had reached this unlikely—sometimes seemingly fantastical—destination because of my willingness to venture into uncharted territory, honoring my heart's deepest desires as expressions of what can be.

———

Magic—uncovering what was just unknowable, creating something extraordinary out of seemingly ordinary ingredients—is what makes me come alive. So my intention heading into an Ayahuasca ceremony was to remove the barriers to creating more magic in my life and in the world. When the medicine came on during the first night, I settled into my typical pattern of grieving, folding my body onto itself and closing my eyes. Then, something within me said to my mom, *I'm tired of being sad about you.* And I sat up straight and opened my eyes.

During the ceremony, I started to understand that I can't create all that I am meant to create if I am always grieving. My body can't do all that it's meant for if I am always hunched over. I wondered, *Wow, am I really done grieving the loss of my mother?* I cautiously accepted this possibility, making way for what's next. Okay, let's make some magic!

But not quite.

Or, at least, not yet.

At the start of the next night's ceremony, I fell into excruciating physical pain, crawling out of my skin. I glanced across the ceremony toward the lead Ayahuasquero, wondering if I could make my way to her for support. I thought about drinking water to help me come down from the high. But I stayed with it, remembering that Mother Aya would not give me more than I could handle. After what felt like hours of misery, I learned that the pain I was feeling was pain that my body had held for me, for decades, until I was ready to look at it. Now it was time. So I surrendered to the pain, and Mother Aya took me to the place to which I had never been able to travel before—to the utter devastation I felt when I lost my mother.

It was like an explosion. I was obliterated into a red galaxy of heartbreak and despair. My body writhed in anguish. I couldn't cry because it was too much to even breathe. As the emotion lightened, I tried to ground myself. I breathed big, labored, groaning breaths. I rubbed my legs over and over. I hugged my body, rocking it back and forth, simultaneously so deeply sorry and so deeply grateful that it had held such monstrous pain without my knowing.

Then Mother Aya asked, "Are you ready?" And we went back in.

Over and over, we ventured to the depths of my pain. The Ayahuasqueros came over several times to sit with me, to hold me, to sing to me. I felt unspeakably grateful for their support, collapsing in their embrace. I felt unspeakably grateful for Mother Aya, for the opportunity to unpack all of this with her instead of all by myself. I felt unspeakably grateful for my father, for my mother's best friend, for all those throughout my life who held things with me, for me, until I could hold them alone.

And, I felt unspeakably grateful for my body.

My body has shielded me from the pain I couldn't bear—my entire life, in every moment. Dissociating to numb my heartbreak when I was young. Holding the pain and the tension for me when it's too much and I escape my body through coping mechanisms. Every time I leave my body through distraction or numbing or planning or managing or bracing, the pain does not disappear—it is stored in my body. And my body wisely, compassionately, patiently holds all of it for me until I am ready.

And when I am ready, when I come back into my body— through grief work, through breathwork, with psychedelics—I open myself to an energetic force of love that moves without my directing it. My brain could not solve the problem of my loneliness and sadness. It was the voice in the woods—a voice that came from within my body—that told me it was time to wake up. My brain rejected my partner on the first pass. It was the voice after my grieving session—a voice that came from within my body—that told me to reach out to him. Despite my brain's skepticism, my body told me during our first hug that it was right. My brain thought I was a terrible writer with nothing to say! It was my body that started typing that early morning, my brain watching with shock and delight.

When I said I was tired of being sad about my mom, I was saying I was ready to face it all. My body can't do what it's meant to do *and* hold all of that unconscious pain for me. So, if I am really ready to step up the magic-making, if I want to access the love and divine wisdom that flow through my body, I need to relieve my body of its pain-holding duties. Not that I'm finished grieving. But the more I can get to the source, the more I can release, the more capacity I free up to bask in and share my loving creativity with the world.

But also—I *might* be done grieving my mom, at least in the same way I used to. After going to the depths of my pain during Ayahuasca, my grief about my mother no longer feels permanent and unbearable. There is more openness, more curiosity, more hopefulness. I had the sense that layers between my mom and me were removed that night—layers that I had unconsciously held onto and finally was able to relinquish. I am on the verge of something here.

As I look back on these last few years, I marvel at how beautifully my life has transformed. But something within me is saying, *You better hold on, Lex. We're just getting started.*

Reflections

Everything I Do Is Right

For years, I watched anxiously how my dryer's lint filter didn't catch all the lint, some falling into the unknowable compartment deep within. I was confident it was accumulating and would someday take over the house. Right after my co-parent—who previously handled these kinds of tasks—moved out, the day of reckoning arrived. The lint error code popped up, so I gathered my courage and my new toolbox and got to work. I uninstalled the lint catcher compartment, vacuumed everything out, and painfully reinstalled it with my inexperienced, contorted body half in the dryer. Sweaty but proud, mission accomplished—minus one lost, surely unimportant screw. But the error code did not disappear! I went to confirm that my interpretation was correct, that the error code CL means "clean lint." (*For fuck's sake, did she just say, "Clean lint"? Wouldn't it be "CF" for "clean filter"?*) Ah, "child lock." Three seconds later, we are up and running!

Once someone told me that everything I do is right. At the time I thought, *Well, that's an annoying thing to say. And that cannot be true.* But I started to see it. We will keep doing what we're doing until we're tired of doing it. And when we continue to resist change, to resist facing our pain, we will create more painful circumstances that will trigger us again and give us another opportunity to face our pain. I heard a voice that helped me see it was time to look inward. Another path may be hitting rock bottom. Rock bottom is not a bad thing! It is a beautiful place of rebirth.

What I love to think is that each time we keep doing things in the old way, in a way that doesn't serve us, we are stockpiling that energy in a bank account. So when we do finally cash in, when we do finally decide to make this change, we are loaded with energy and ready to go. I was so frustrated that it took me nineteen years in my relationship with my co-parent to figure out what I needed. Nineteen years! What if I could have figured this out in the first few and saved myself all of this pain? Or be so much further down the path? But the rapid expansion I have experienced in the last few years was cashing in on that stored energy. I got to the place I was going to get to—it just took the shape of a slow, steady ramp up and then a burst at the end.

And—I think there's more to this encouraging statement. It is an optical illusion of sorts. When I'm having a difficult moment, I'll say to myself, *This is the work, Alexis. You are doing amazing work.* And then something transforms. It gives me permission to be exactly where I am. And not needing to be elsewhere lets me sink into my body. I surrender, I become pliable. Maybe in the moment before, I was stuck in a recurring thought pattern. Maybe my energy was dispersed, with worries about others, with worries about tomorrow. Maybe I was dismantling my dryer when all that was needed was pushing a button. But if I gain just enough consciousness to accept myself as I am, where I am, I relax into my body and open myself up to the infinite love and wisdom that flow through me, always.

Spiritual Laundry

One Friday night after a long, unusually busy week with terrible sleep, I was doing my best to wrap things up and get my kiddo and me to bed. I had been washing my sheets and duvet cover and hoping to get them dry for bedtime. But when I went to move things to the dryer, I noticed water everywhere. The washer's drain hose had detached from the wall. So I got out the towels and did my best to move the washer, dryer, and fridge around so I could get to the water underneath. Okay, crisis managed. It's late—I gotta get this kid to bed. Then I'll stay up and make my bed when the dry cycle is done.

But when he got into bed, I noticed a wet spot on his blanket.

"Did you spill water?"

"I don't think so."

"Well you had to have—otherwise, what would this be?"

Cat urine. Exhausted and my patience having been used up on the earlier mini crisis, the f-bombs flowed easily. Strip everything, get it into the fucking wash, and make sure that fucking hose is adequately reattached.

"Okay, you're sleeping in the guest bed tonight."

We had a sweet cuddle session, and because it was too late to deal with my bed by this time, I just fell asleep in the guest bed too.

Four forty-five in the morning: I hear my son scratching. More scratching. So much scratching.

I shoot out of bed, realizing that the lice that have been making their way around his class have finally shown themselves to us. (Are you itching now? You're welcome.)

I launch into all of the to-dos. Check for lice. Treat for lice. Call one of those companies that treats for lice to catch the ones I didn't get. Wash all the sheets and blankets and stuffies and clothes. Some stuff goes in the dishwasher. Other stuff goes in the freezer. Quarantine everything else for weeks and weeks. Vacuum every goddamn inch of the house.

I am spiritual until I have a to-do list—at the bottom of the to-do list is to become spiritual again when everything is done. But I do not want to cope! I do not want to make this anxiety go away by doing. I want to stay with the anxiety so I don't miss the gems that are being offered here.

So on this early morning, as my son slept, I sat on the beige rug in the hall outside the guest bedroom and did my central channel breathing to move the energy that presented as tightness in my chest. I'd breathe and breathe—and then google some stuff about lice—and then get back to breathing and breathing.

And then my energy transformed. From feeling stressed about everything I had to do and fearful that I wouldn't do it perfectly and would have lice forever and ever—to knowing I am safe and delighting in the ridiculous set of unfolding laundry-related circumstances. My cat didn't want to be outshined by the lice in this laundry charade. She wanted to preempt their reveal so she could see her impact on the world too. And if all the beds weren't out of commission, I wouldn't have had the opportunity to sleep right next to my son to share this head-scratching experience.

This was a benign set of circumstances involving some benign creatures. And it still can cause so much suffering if I received it as if it's happening to me, it's an obstacle to my plans, it's unrelated to or separate from what I'm on this earth to do. It is exactly what I'm on this earth to do! Everything that triggers me is offering a deeper truth about how safe and loved I am.

Even lice and cat urine.

No Reflection

My partner does not always respond to my texts, and this was very triggering for me early on. I would send a text and would not receive even an acknowledgment of receipt, let alone confirmation that what I sent was of value. My immediate interpretation was that what I said must not have been interesting enough, funny enough. That is, this was my younger part's interpretation, and she would freak out almost immediately after the text left my phone in anticipation of a negative or lacking response.

My practice to work through this in the most intense moments was to put my hand on my heart and actually talk out loud to this part: "I know, it's so scary to put yourself out there and not get feedback from the other that you are seen and appreciated. But you are lovely just as you are, regardless of the feedback or lack thereof from others. And you are so courageous, continuing to pursue love after so much hurt. What a beautiful gift you offer to others. You will find your way to those who see and appreciate you just as you are."

It helped, and she would calm down. Over time, I have learned that my partner's lack of response does not indicate the value he takes away from my communication—we just have different styles. And I have learned that it matters most how I enjoy and value my communication. I like my sense of humor, my warmth, my vulnerability. I am fed by this and don't need someone else to validate it.

When there is a void of reflection from another, it leaves me only with my own sense. And when my sense is shaky, I fill in that lack of reflection with a negative, perhaps worst-case perspective. And when you write a book and start sending some pages to friends and family and you don't get a response back, one of the possibilities (so I hear) is that you believe you are Russell Crowe's character from *A Beautiful Mind* and that what makes sense to you, what lights you up, is complete gibberish to others. Frankly, maybe it is.

Each of us carries a unique shade of divinity. That's one thing I loved so much when I started waking up. Realizing that my spreadsheet-building, burlesque-dancing, electronica-loving, cursing self is one to be celebrated as just right—not an outcast while everyone else is in the same right bucket. We are all so different—and just right.

So maybe my work resonates with many, and maybe it resonates with no one. The critical piece is whether it resonates with me. Does it fill me up? Do I love what I create?

My Toolbox

As I was reading *The Wisdom Wheel* by Alberto Villoldo, I came to a meditation where you journey to "the Island of Sacred Animals." The idea is that you find yourself on this island, and your power animal will be revealed to you.

I could not imagine this to be true—I am a skeptic!—but I followed the meditation. I paddled to the island via canoe and walked through the forest into a clearing, where I was sure no power animal would actually meet me. And then, right in the middle of the clearing, a cheetah's penetrating eyes met mine. I started bawling. It resonated so deeply. For a long while after, every time I went on a run, a cheetah ran right next to me, grounding me and propelling me forward.

Whether power animals are real and whether the cheetah is mine, I am open either way. What I know is that this exercise moved me, awakened something within me. There are so many spiritual tools available—yoga, chants, sound healing, crystals, horoscopes, tarot, visualizations, connecting with the elements, eating intentionally—the list goes on! What I understand is that I don't have to do any of these spiritual exercises, and that is just right. And if I am called to do these exercises, that is just right. It's not important to me to know what's real about angels and power animals and alternate lifetimes. For me, everything is about resonance, about finding the truth within. And all of these tools are just there, available to point to the truth if I find them useful. This can go both ways! If someone's teaching resonates, that points to something that feels true within me. And if someone's teaching doesn't resonate, that also points to what feels true within me. Everything is shining a light.

I had the opportunity to try out an Ayurvedic anointment practice where you apply oil and herb blends to specific channels, which are doorways between consciousness and our physical bodies. I felt relaxed and peaceful after. My brain cannot accept without proof that this practice does what it says it does, but it can accept that slowing down and attending to my body with presence and gentle touch was a loving act that changed me. When I can let go of who and what is right or wrong, finding the evidence for my thinking brain, I can just follow what resonates and trust I am on the right track, trust that I am finding more truth—even when my brain can't quite grasp it.

It's All for You

When my partner and I were just bringing our families together, we all spent a few days together in Italy. Coming into this gathering, I was stressed and exhausted. The journey to Europe had taken twenty-four hours with delays, and while my son was a champ—pinching me to keep me awake on that first day!—I was not operating at my best. And I felt a lot of pressure bringing the kids together, anxious to see how everyone would get along.

We stayed in Positano for a couple of days in a hotel right on the beach. The room my son and I stayed in had the cutest tile work in white and turquoise and a view of the bay. It was hot while we were there, so I opened the window to try to cool down the room at night. As the many yachts parked in the bay were partying all night long with very loud music, I genuinely appreciated the fun they were having—and, fuck, I wished for a little sleep so I could be more rested going into the next day. I needed to fill my tank. But that was not in the cards, so I slept a little on and off throughout the night.

And then, around five in the morning, I heard a saxophone. And what sounded like musical instruments being tuned. *That's strange,* I thought. Then I heard the most beautiful classical music piece. It sounded like live music, but that made no sense. I went to look out the window but couldn't see anything beyond the hotel roof. It must just be a very high quality speaker, I guess! I was soothed by this music, and another piece followed, and then another. At some point, these beautiful pieces coaxed me into a deep slumber.

When we met up with my partner and his kids later that morning, he told me how he saw maybe one hundred people in tuxes and formal wear in line for coffee at six in the morning. *Holy shit.* This gorgeous, soothing music that rocked me to sleep was a full, live symphony, playing on the beach in Positano at five in the morning. We wondered what they were possibly doing. Maybe practicing before going to perform for someone on one of the nearby islands? We never figured it out. But we didn't need to—I know they played for me. They gave this beautiful gift to anyone who could take it in.

When I go out for a run and I see all the gorgeous fall colors, I now know all of that's for me. I used to think that was egotistical—it can't possibly be for me, one of the billions of people on earth. But once I realize I am not me,

I am the universe, I am everything in one person, that we are all connected, that we are all the same divinity—then it does get to all be for me. It is, every piece of goodness, for me. Taking it in lets me more deeply tap into how much I'm loved and how much I am love and how much love I have to give others. Love that others don't need from me once they realize that they are god, that they are love, that every piece of goodness in this life is for them.

I once dropped off flowers for a friend who was struggling, signing the card, "With love from the universe." And she quipped, "These are not from the universe, they are from you."

Ah, but I am the universe. There is no love that is not the universe. The love that planted and nurtured these beautiful flowers, that harvested them and delivered them to the store, that picked them out just for you—all of this was a channel bringing the goodness that is meant for you to you. A channel of love that will unceasingly flow around and within you, and one day, dear one, you will wake up to it.

From Stillness

I sat still a lot as a kid. I sat in front of the TV. I sat with my sleeping mother. I sat at my kitchen table, hoping to intersect with my loved ones. I sat outside of school or extracurriculars when I was forgotten. I sat in fear in my living room when I was home alone, terrified that someone was going to abduct me.

When I grew up, I kept sitting still. I stayed home. I didn't know where to go or what to do or how to meet people. I didn't know what I liked, so travel didn't make sense to me. Go somewhere *meh* with all of the downsides—getting stuck, getting sick? The risks of wandering out into the world seemed to greatly outweigh the benefits. So I watched more TV. Long hours on my couch with my laptop for work and law school studies.

And when I had my own kid, I didn't have enough energy to run around with him, to climb the boulders, to venture into the river, so I'd sit still, looking on as he and my co-parent adventured.

Now my life is one of movement. I'm running sprints around the track while my son's team practices. I'm scaling the fence to retrieve the errant soccer ball. After his game, as parents file into the single line up the stairs, I bound up the grass hill with the kids. I'm giggling while doing push-ups on the playground, as I discover that several elementary-age humans have come to join me. I am in a constant state of laughter as I get pummeled by dodgeballs, as I await discovery during hide-and-seek. I travel to beautiful locales to hike and run and kayak and paddleboard. I fly to Maui regularly to meditate in the early morning amidst the palm trees, with the moon still high, reflecting on the ocean below.

When I tell people what I'm up to, something lights up in them. They start writing that book they've always wanted to write. A friend heard about the trips I take to Maui, and she said, "I'd love to do that."

I asked, "What's keeping you from doing it?"

"I don't know," she responded. A month later I learned she took her first solo trip to Hawaii.

When we care for ourselves, we give permission to others to take care of themselves. When we start to come to life, it can't not awaken something in those around us. My aliveness spills out into the world, dwarfing the pale, timid, teeny contributions I could muster from my place of sadness and stillness.

And yet—I heard the voice in the woods in my sadness and stillness. Was my life so quiet, so slow, so still that I could hear? There is a sense that what I was doing before was not good and what I am doing now is good. But are they one and the same? What I was doing before led to what I am doing now. There is no *this* without *that*. The silence and stillness were the seeds planted that would blossom into this vibrant, love-filled life.

Breadcrumbs

When I was working through my divorce paperwork, I felt saddened that I didn't have any family members there with me. I was finalizing one of the biggest decisions of my life, and I was sitting alone at my dining table. I specifically missed my mother, which was surprising because I don't remember feeling that way around my wedding or the birth of my child. But now, I wanted my mom there to make me tea.

Then, without any conscious thought, something within my body said, *I'll do that for you.*

And for the next round of paperwork, I bought myself flowers and made myself tea and felt held.

During a period of writer's block, my editor walked me through an exercise where I settled into my body and asked this book what it wanted to be. The book said it would make me tea, that it was here to nourish me. It said that it was my gift to me. I have wondered about that. In July 2020, I heard a voice that said if I died that day, my life would have been a tragedy. So is this book my message to that younger me—my message of hope, of transformation, of a lovelier life?

After writing the bulk of this book, I would still have episodes of intense sadness, of heartbreak, of deeply painful emotions, during which I felt lost and untethered. During one of these dark nights of the soul, I craved support and began to reach out to others who had helped me in the past. But I needed support, like, *now*. And then I remembered my book, that it said it was for me.

So I came back and read my book. And it was the guidance and support I was desperately needing, holding me as I felt gutted, reminding me of the truths I had discovered before, helping me feel so deeply loved.

My default is to think linearly—that the younger version of me must not be as wise as the older version of me, as I gain more wisdom with time. But holy moly, am I grateful for the younger Alexis who came before and wrote all of this, the one who was so connected with the wisdom of the universe and the infinite love that surrounds me always, the one who could lend her insights and love to the later me who was back in the depths of the hard work.

Rumi laments our tendency to look outside ourselves— we look for drops from others, yet we have a fountain within. We seek crusts from others, unaware of our own basket of fresh bread. I have left myself breadcrumbs through this writing, through my recorded dance videos, through the voice memos of my singing and my piano compositions. When I lose connection with the love and strength and magic I have within, I can follow these breadcrumbs to remind me, to lead me back to my basket of bread.

We each have unique, extraordinary gifts to share with the world, but most importantly to feed and to remind ourselves. These gifts are our remembrance of the divine.

Emotion Doula

I am not done feeling heart-wrenching pain. But when it comes up, I now feel it with tools, I feel it with support. My higher self holds my part that feels that pain—I no longer hold it alone. And I bear it with the knowing that I am about to embark on something so beautiful, previously unfathomable. When I began to be able to feel everything, pain became a portal to beauty, and previously numbed joy came through with total clarity.

But when the pain returns, I am immersed in it. I feel broken, and I don't think I can come back from it. It can feel so overwhelming. So I've written myself a script. I have had the sense that having something to hold on to, something to return to when I get these overwhelming emotional experiences might help me. So I share that here in case it could help you too.

Hi, my love. I see that you are feeling so much heartbreak / anger / desperation / panic / fear / disappointment / frustration / _____ right now. This is the moment! Your body is telling you that you are ready—right now—for transformation. If you feel the depth of this emotion, you will set it free and find something exquisite in its stead.

This is the time to pause your interactions with the outside world. The outside world played its part by triggering you, and now is the time for you to travel inward.

As you can, give your brain a break and allow the wisdom of the body and the soul to direct you. As to the stories that keep wanting to pop up to protect you, you can lovingly welcome them in. Sometimes these stories can help us deepen our feeling of this emotion. And when you are ready, you can set them down, as they are not truth. Truth will be revealed on the other side, and you will know what to do.

I am right here with you, holding you, loving you as you embark on this profound journey. You are birthing more love into your body, into the world. Feeling your emotion fully is the portal to a new, larger, more wondrous life. I know it can feel like you will get stuck here. It can feel like there is no other reality but the one you feel right now. But this is just a moment in time, an emotion that will move on if you let it. My brave, dear one, you are almost there. And at every step, I am right here with you, holding you, loving you.

Acknowledgments

To those who follow—and to the countless others who have helped me discover more of who I am—I offer my deepest gratitude.

To my childhood community. To my dear friends, who surrounded me with kindness and compassion. To their parents, who graciously welcomed me into their homes. To my schoolteachers, whose nurturing gave me comfort, whose reflections gave me glimpses of my goodness. To my mother's best friend, whose love and warmth were my beacon of light.

To my grown-up community. To Katie and Jessie for their grounding wisdom and loving support. To Evie Graham and Vega Dance+Lab for helping me delight in my body after so many years of escaping it. To Mike and Caryn for creating the special environment where the bulk of this book was written.

To my editors. To Brianna McCabe, who was the first to see the potential in my work and was my biggest, unwavering cheerleader as I wrote and then whittled down hundreds of thousands of words! To Carmen Riot Smith, whose diligence and clarity helped me become diligent and clear, who identified gaps in my story that ultimately represented opportunities to find deeper understanding and healing.

To my teachers and healers. To my therapists, who held me with such gentleness as I began to wake up to my pain. To Katherine Woodward Thomas and Melody Beattie, whose books helped me find a new way of being. To Christina Marlett, Marci Shimoff, and Dr. Sue Morter for their loving, life-changing teachings and guidance. To the plant medicines and my extraordinary guides, for their unspeakable power and intelligence and magnificence.

To Maui, whose sands have received my tears on so many occasions, whose waves have washed away the pieces that no longer serve, whose moon and stars have shone down on me to illuminate a path forward.

To my father and my sisters, who loved me throughout my life, who supported me when I couldn't yet support myself. For their inspiring, incredible displays of perseverance and strength.

To my co-parent, who stood by my side as I unknowingly carried such monstrous pain. Who said the most beautiful three words to me when I was not yet strong enough to face my abandonment pain: "I'm still here." And who gave me the most precious gift, our son.

To my partner, whose playfulness, tenderness, strength, and aliveness invite me to be playful, tender, strong and alive. And who has shared his two most precious gifts with me.

To my son, the light of my life.

To my mother, whom I miss so much.

I am forever and inexpressibly grateful.

About the Author

Alexis Leigh is an investment banker turned seeker from Texas and brings her warm Texan storytelling to her debut memoir, *Pain Is a Portal to Beauty*. Not one to follow the beaten path, Alexis has relentlessly examined what she learned from others against her own experience and offers a fresh take to many topics, from internal family systems to romantic love. She has a knack for connecting the dots, translating big bodies of work into something accessible, grounded in the practical. When not writing at her local coffee shop, Alexis can be found meditating under the stars on Maui or finding adventure with her partner and their three boys. Alexis lives in Oregon.